# Using
# Excel 2019

D1567516

## Kevin Wilson

Elluminet Press
www.elluminetpress.com

# Using Excel 2019

Publisher: Elluminet Press
Director: Kevin Wilson
Lead Editor: Steven Ashmore
Technical Reviewer: Mike Taylor, Robert Ashcroft
Copy Editors: Joanne Taylor, James Marsh
Proof Reader: Mike Taylor
Indexer: James Marsh
Cover Designer: Kevin Wilson

eBook versions and licenses are also available for most titles. Any source code or other supplementary materials referenced by the author in this text is available to readers at

www.elluminetpress.com/resources

For detailed information about how to locate your book's resources, go to

www.elluminetpress.com/resources

# Table of Contents

# About the Author

With over 15 years' experience in the computer industry, Kevin Wilson has made a career out of technology and showing others how to use it. After earning a master's degree in computer science, software engineering, and multimedia systems, Kevin has held various positions in the IT industry including graphic & web design, building & managing corporate networks, training, and IT support.

He currently serves as Elluminet Press Ltd's senior writer and director, he periodically teaches computer science at college in South Africa and serves as an IT trainer in England. His books have become a valuable resource among the students in England, South Africa and our partners in the United States.

Kevin's motto is clear: "If you can't explain something simply, then you haven't understood it well enough." To that end, he has created a series of textbooks, in which he breaks down complex technological subjects into smaller, easy-to-follow steps that students and ordinary computer users can put into practice.

# Spreadsheets

Microsoft Excel is a spreadsheet program that allows you to store, organize, analyse and manipulate numerical data. It allows you to store and present it in tabular form or as a chart.

You can use spreadsheets to create wage slips, company accounts to analyse finance, budgets and present information.

You can create simple personal budgets to keep track of your money, and create score sheets for sports events.

You can display all your data as statistical graphs and charts as well as creating tables.

To begin lets explore what a spreadsheet is.

# What is a Spreadsheet?

A spreadsheet is made up of cells each identified by a reference. The reference is made up by using the column, eg D, and the row, eg 10

[COLUMN] [ROW]

So the highlighted cell would be D10 as illustrated below.

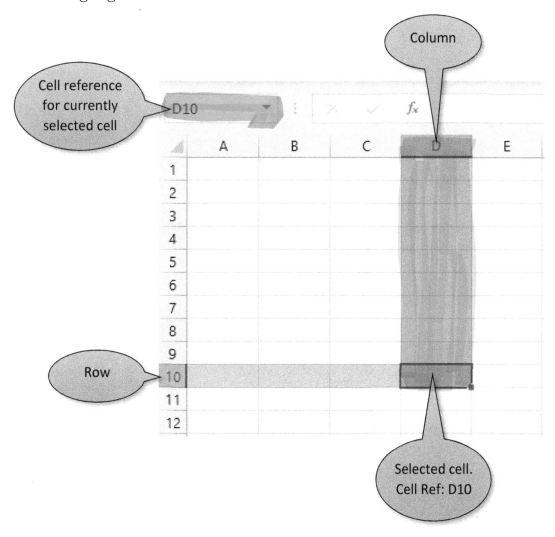

You can also select multiple cells at the same time. A group of cells is called as a cell range.

You can refer to a cell range, using the cell reference of the first cell and the last cell in the range, separated by a colon.

[FIRST CELL in RANGE] : [LAST CELL in RANGE]

## Chapter 1: Spreadsheets

For example, this cell range would be A1:D10 (firstcell : lastcell).

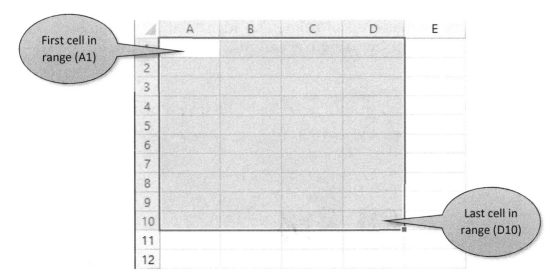

Cell references are used when you start applying functions to the numbers in your cells.

In the example below, to add two numbers together, you can enter a formula into cell C1.

Instead of typing in **=5+5** you would enter **=A1+B1**.

The theory is, if you enter the cell reference instead of the actual number, you can perform calculations automatically and Excel will recalculate all the numbers for you should you change anything.

For example, if I wanted to change it to **5+6**, I would just change the number in cell B1 without rewriting the formula in C1.

Now you can type any number in either cell A1 or B1 and it will add them up automatically.

This is a very basic example but forms the building blocks of a spreadsheet. You can use these concepts to build spreadsheets to analyse and manipulate data, as well as allow changes to the individual data and other parts of the spreadsheet without constantly changing formulas and functions.

You can analyse your data using pivot tables, goal seek and scenario manager.

| Recommended Retail Price | | |
|---|---|---|
| **Revenues** | | |
| Price per Book | £ | 14.95 |
| Book Sales | | 50 |
| **Total revenue** | £ | 747.50 |
| | | |
| **Expenditure** | | |
| RRP | | 14.95 |
| Discount | | 55% |
| Wholesale Price | £ | 6.73 |
| Total Stock | | 50 |
| **Total Cost** | £ | 336.38 |
| | | |
| **Profit Margin** | £ | 411.13 |

| Sale Price | | |
|---|---|---|
| **Revenues** | | |
| Price per Book | £ | 10.95 |
| Book Sales | | 50 |
| **Total revenue** | £ | 547.50 |
| | | |
| **Expenditure** | | |
| RRP | | 14.95 |
| Discount | | 55% |
| Wholesale Price | £ | 6.73 |
| Total Stock | | 50 |
| **Total Cost** | £ | 336.38 |
| | | |
| **Profit Margin** | £ | 211.13 |

| Give Away Price | | |
|---|---|---|
| **Revenues** | | |
| Price per Book | £ | 8.99 |
| Book Sales | | 50 |
| **Total revenue** | £ | 449.50 |
| | | |
| **Expenditure** | | |
| RRP | | 14.95 |
| Discount | | 55% |
| Wholesale Price | £ | 6.73 |
| Total Stock | | 50 |
| **Total Cost** | £ | 336.38 |
| | | |
| **Profit Margin** | £ | 113.13 |

You can also create charts to visually represent your data.

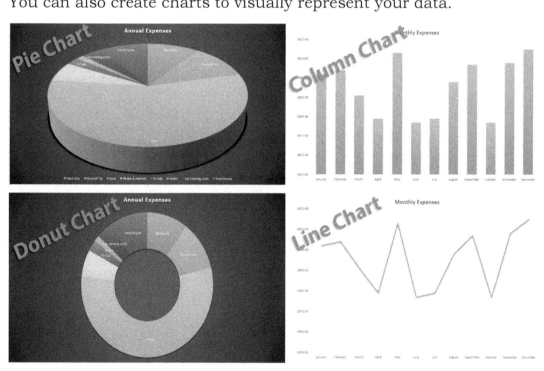

We'll take a look at these features later in the book.

# Getting Started with Excel

In this section, we'll take a look at starting Excel and a tour of the main screen.

# Starting Excel

The quickest way to start Microsoft Excel is to search for it using the Cortana search field on the bottom left of your task bar. Type 'excel' into the search field. From the search results click 'excel'. You'll also find Excel on your start menu.

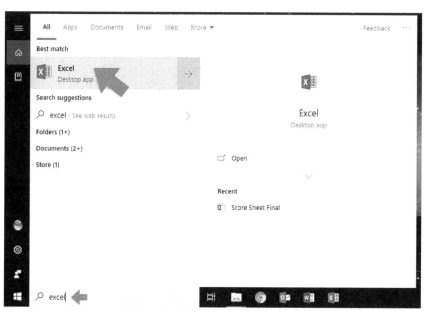

Once Excel has started, you'll land on the home screen. On the home screen, you'll see recently used templates along the top, and your most recently saved spreadsheets listed underneath.

To begin, click 'blank workbook' to start. This will open up Excel with a new spreadsheet for you.

# Main Screen

Once you have selected a template, you will see your main screen.

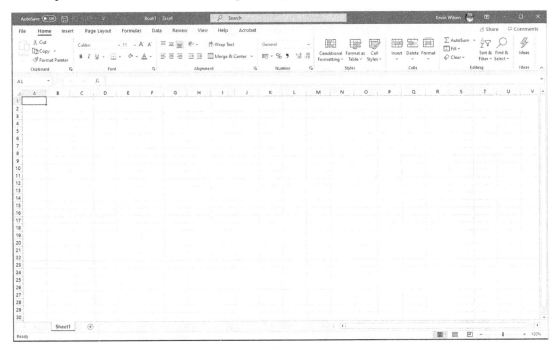

Your columns are labelled across the top of your worksheet with letters and your rows are labelled down the left hand side with numbers. These make up cell references that we'll look at later.

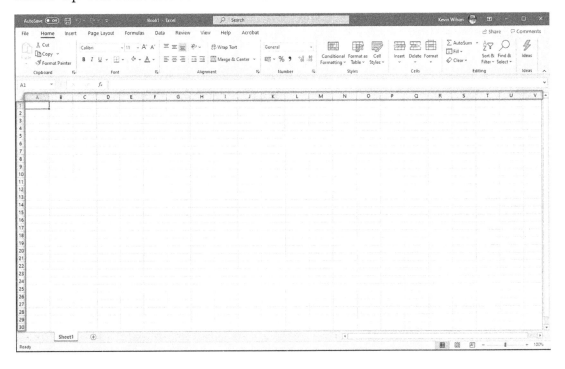

Underneath the ribbon menu, you'll see a cell reference and next to that the formula bar.

Across the bottom of the screen on the left hand side, you'll see some tabs. This shows you all the worksheets you have created in your workbook - you can click these to switch to that worksheet. You can create a new worksheet here, if you click the small plus icon next to the tabs.

On the bottom right, you can change how Excel displays your worksheet. Grid view is your normal view as shown above, print view shows you how your spreadsheet will look when printed.

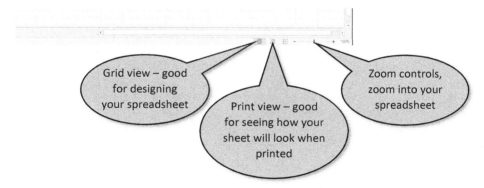

Further to the right you have your zoom controls. This allows you to zoom in and out of your spreadsheet.

# Chapter 2: Getting Started with Excel

You can either use the slider to zoom in and out, or you can click on the 'zoom percentage' on the bottom right.

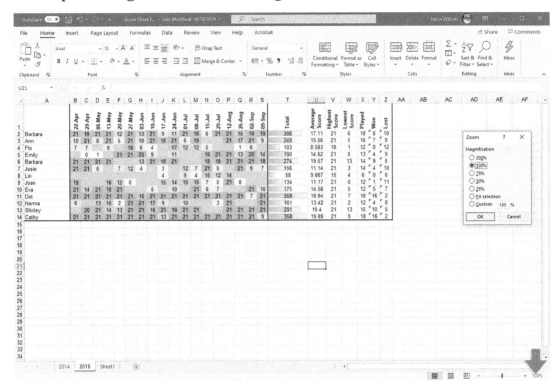

From the 'zoom' dialog box that appears, you can select the zoom level.

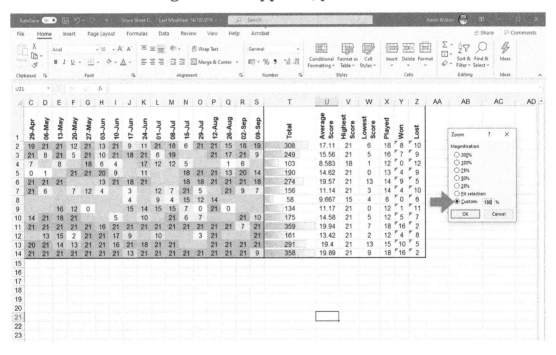

Click 'ok' when you're done.

**16**

# The Ribbon

All the tools used in Microsoft Excel are organised into a ribbon which is divided into ribbon tabs, each containing a specific set of tools.

The most used ribbon tabs are home, insert and formulas. For normal use of Excel, these are the ones you will be looking in the most detail.

## The Home Ribbon Tab

This is where you will find your most used tools for basic text formatting, cell borders, cell formatting for text and numbers or currency, etc.

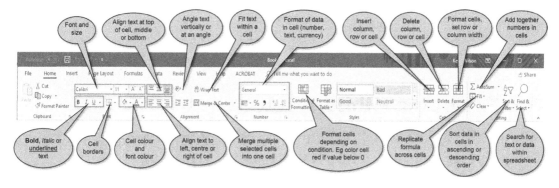

## The Insert Ribbon Tab

This is where you will find all your objects that you can insert into your spreadsheet, such as shapes, tables and charts.

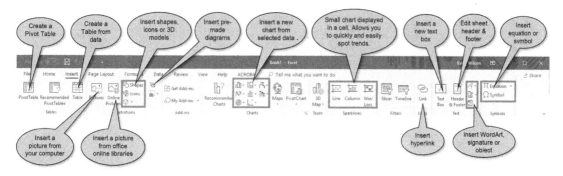

You can also insert equations and symbols, as well as pivot tables and pivot charts.

# The Page Layout Ribbon Tab

This is where you will find your page formatting functions, such as size of paper, colours & themes, paper orientation when printed, paper margins, etc.

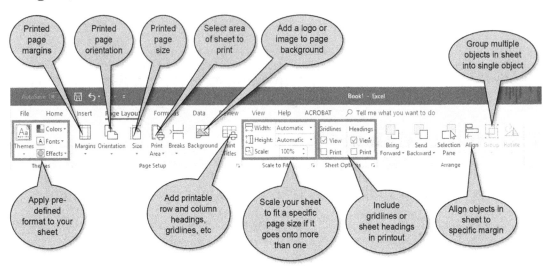

# The Formulas Ribbon Tab

This is where you will find your formulas, functions and your data manipulation tools. Sum functions, average, counting tools, etc.

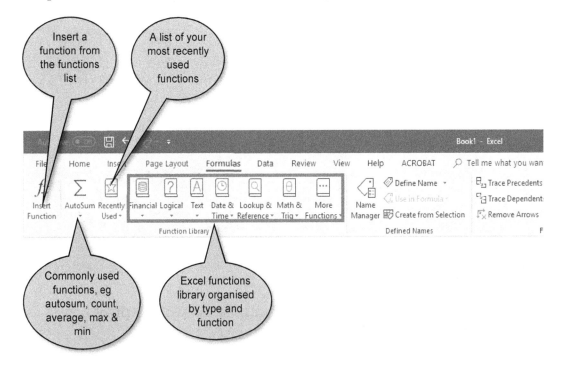

# The Data Ribbon Tab

The data ribbon is where you can find tools to connect to external data sources and databases, as well as sort data.

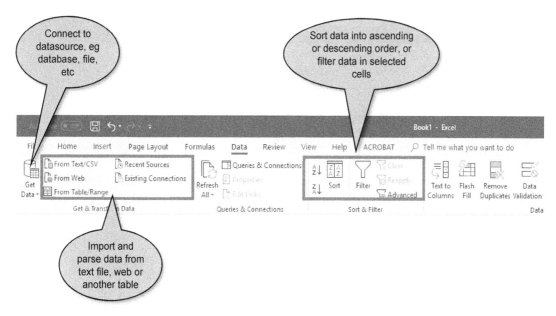

# The Review Ribbon Tab

The review ribbon has tools that allow you to add comments as well as check spelling and protect parts of the spreadsheet from making changes.

# The View Ribbon Tab

This is where you will find your view layouts, where you can zoom into your spreadsheet etc.

# File Backstage

If you click 'File' on the top left of your screen, this will open up what Microsoft call the backstage.

Backstage is where you open or save spreadsheets and workbooks, print, export or share workbooks, as well as options, Microsoft account and preference settings.

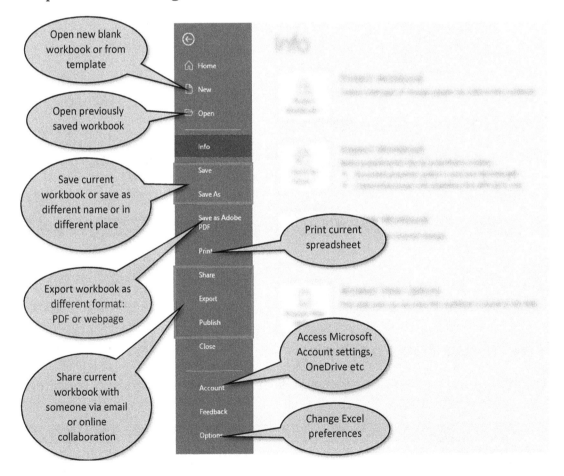

You can also change your Microsoft Account settings, log in and activate your Microsoft Office, change Excel's preferences and so on.

# Tell Me Feature

Microsoft has added a feature to Office that allows you to search for commands and tools in any of the Office Applications.

You can find this field on the top right of the screen. Here it is pictured in Excel.

Type a command in to the field. For example, if I wanted to insert a picture, type 'insert picture' into the search field.

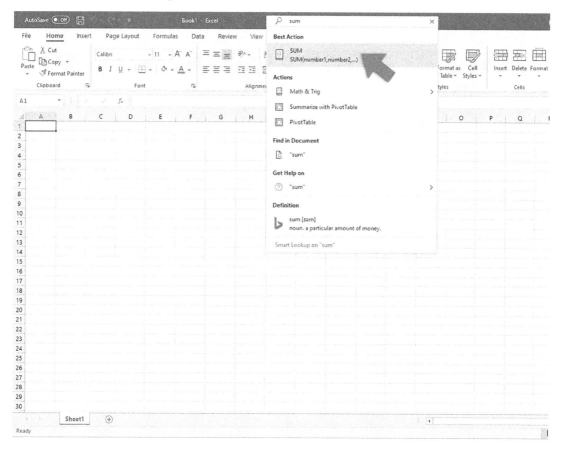

From the drop down menu that appears, click on the command you were looking for.

This feature can be used in all the Office Apps. If you can't find the tool on the menus or ribbons, just search for it.

# Building Spreadsheets

In this section, we'll take a look at building and formatting spreadsheets.

Before we begin, throughout this section, we will be using the resource files.

You can download these files from

`www.elluminetpress.com/ms-excel`

Go down to the files section and click the icons to download the documents to the documents folder on your PC.

# Creating a New Workbook

To create a new blank workbook, click 'file' on the top left of your screen,

Select 'new', then double click the 'blank workbook' thumbnail.

You'll see a blank spreadsheet where you can start to enter your data.

# Entering Data

In this example we are doing a basic scoring sheet. To enter data, click on the cell you want, then type in the data.

| | A | B | C | D |
|---|---|---|---|---|
| 1 | | 22-Apr | 29-Apr | Total |
| 2 | Barbara | 21 | 19 | |
| 3 | Ann | 10 | 21 | |
| 4 | Flo | 7 | 7 | |
| 5 | Rose | 9 | 12 | |
| 6 | Emily | | 0 | |
| 7 | Josie | 21 | 21 | |
| 8 | Lin | | | |
| 9 | Joan | 19 | | |
| 10 | Eva | 21 | 14 | |
| 11 | | | | |

# Simple Text Formatting

Sometimes it improves the readability of your spreadsheet to format the data in the cells.

For example, make the heading rows bold.

You can do this by selecting the heading row as shown above and click the bold icon.

# Text Orientation

Now because the headings are quite long and take up a lot of space, you can change the orientation of the headings to read vertically instead of horizontally. This helps save space and looks better when printed on a page.

To do this, select the cells you want to change the orientation of. Then right click your mouse on the selection. From the menu that appears, select 'format cells'.

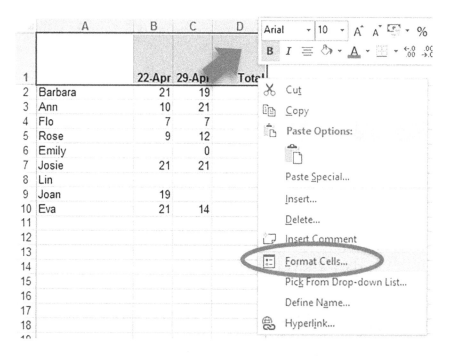

In the dialog box, click the alignment tab. From there, go to the orientation section on the right of the dialog box.

Click the horizontal point (circled above) and drag it up to the top (the vertical point). Or you can enter 90 in the degrees box.

You will see the headings are now oriented vertically.

# Resizing Rows and Columns

You can resize a column or row by clicking and dragging the column or row divider lines as circled below

You can also double click on these lines to automatically size the row or column to the data that is in the cell.

# Inserting Rows & Columns

To insert a row between Flo and Rose, right click with your mouse on the row Rose is in. In this case row 5

| A5 | | $f_x$ | Rose | |

| | A | B 22-Apr | C 29-Apr | D Total |
|---|---|---|---|---|
| 1 | | | | |
| 2 | Barbara | 21 | 19 | |
| 3 | Ann | 10 | 21 | |
| 4 | Flo | 7 | 7 | |
| 5 | Rose | 9 | 12 | |
| 6 | Emily | | 0 | |
| 7 | Josie | 21 | 21 | |
| 8 | Lin | | | |
| 9 | Joan | 19 | | |
| 10 | Eva | 21 | 14 | |

From the menu, click insert. This will insert a blank row above Rose.

Here we can see Excel has inserted a blank row between the players Flo and Rose.

| | A | B (22-Apr) | C (29-Apr) | D (Total) |
|---|---|---|---|---|
| 1 | | | | |
| 2 | Barbara | 21 | 19 | |
| 3 | Ann | 10 | 21 | |
| 4 | Flo | 7 | 7 | |
| 5 | | | | |
| 6 | Rose | 9 | 12 | |
| 7 | Emily | | 0 | |
| 8 | Josie | 21 | 21 | |
| 9 | Lin | | | |

Remember, the new row is always added above the one selected, and a new column is always added before the one selected.

To insert a column it is exactly the same procedure, except you select a column instead of a row.

| | A | B (22-Apr) | C (29-Apr) |
|---|---|---|---|
| 1 | | | |
| 2 | Barbara | 21 | 19 |
| 3 | Ann | 10 | 21 |
| 4 | Flo | 7 | 7 |
| 5 | Rose | 9 | 12 |
| 6 | Emily | | 0 |
| 7 | Josie | 21 | 21 |
| 8 | Lin | | |
| 9 | Joan | 19 | |
| 10 | Eva | 21 | 14 |
| 11 | | | |
| 12 | | | |
| 13 | | | |
| 14 | | | |

# Cut, Copy & Paste

You can copy and paste a cell or cell range and paste it into another worksheet/workbook or in a different location on the same worksheet.

For this example, open **Score Sheet Final.xlsx**. To perform a basic copy, select the cells you want to copy, and from your home ribbon, click copy.

Click the cell where you want the cells to be copied to. I'm going to paste the cells at the end of the table. From your home ribbon, click paste.

By default, Excel pastes everything copied from the selected cells. Sometimes you only want to paste certain things, such as formatting, or just the text or just the formulas. You can do this with the 'paste special' feature.

To find 'paste special', click the small down arrow under the 'paste' icon, on your home ribbon. You'll see a drop down menu with a few options, shown in the illustrations below.

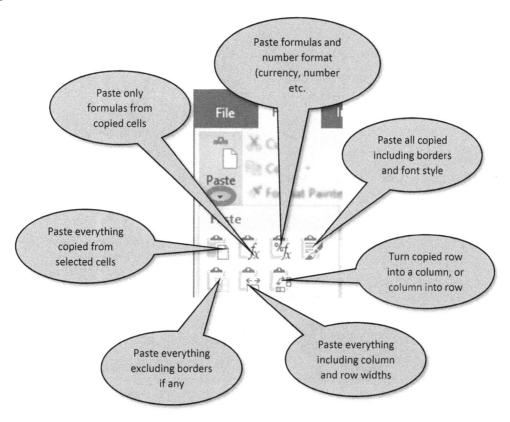

To paste only the formulas, click the second icon across (*fx*).

If you just wanted the values, look further down the drop down menu to the values section, and click '123'.

Finally, if you just wanted the formatting, such as the cell borders and number formatting (currency, number, text etc.), then further down the drop down menu, you'll find the 'other paste options' section. To only paste the formatting, click the first option (%).

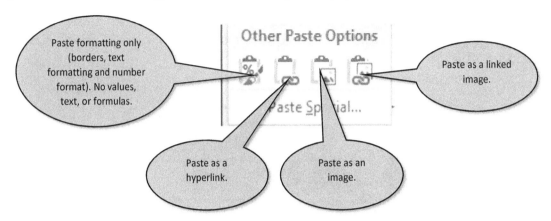

Paste as link can be useful if you are copying and pasting values from a different worksheet to a summarised table. The pasted cells are linked to the copied cells. So if you change the values in the copied cells, they will change in the pasted cells.

| | A | B 22-Apr | C 29-Apr | D Played | E Total | F Average | G Fee |
|---|---|---|---|---|---|---|---|
| 1 | | | | | | | |
| 2 | Barbara | 3 | 19 | 2 | 22 | 11.00 | £ 4.50 |
| 3 | Ann | 10 | 21 | 2 | 31 | 15.50 | £ 4.50 |
| 4 | Flo | 7 | 7 | 2 | 14 | 7.00 | £ 4.50 |
| 5 | Rose | 9 | 12 | 2 | 21 | 10.50 | £ 4.50 |
| 6 | Emily | | 0 | 1 | 0 | 0.00 | £ 4.50 |
| 7 | Josie | 21 | 21 | 2 | 42 | 21.00 | £ 4.50 |
| 8 | Lin | | | 0 | 0 | 0.00 | £ 4.50 |
| 9 | Joan | 19 | | 1 | 19 | 19.00 | £ 4.50 |
| 10 | Eva | 21 | 14 | 2 | 35 | 17.50 | £ 4.50 |
| 11 | | | | | | | |
| 12 | | | | | | | |
| 13 | Barbara | 3 | 19 | 2 | 22 | 11 | 4.5 |

Using 'cut' is exactly the same, except select 'cut' from the home ribbon, instead of copy. The cut command moves the selected cells rather than copying them.

# Sorting Data

To quick sort your data, click on a cell in the column you want to sort the data by. In this example, I want to sort the data by total score so I can see who won this year's player of the year.

Click in the 'total' column. Make sure you click one of the numbers as we want to sort the data, not the title.

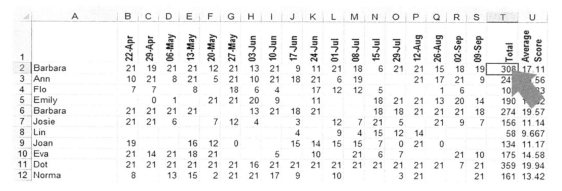

From your home ribbon, click 'sort & filter'. From the drop down menu, click 'Largest to Smallest' (descending order), as we want the highest score listed first.

Looks like Dot won this one...

| | 22-Apr | 29-Apr | 06-May | 13-May | 20-May | 27-May | 03-Jun | 10-Jun | 17-Jun | 24-Jun | 01-Jul | 08-Jul | 15-Jul | 29-Jul | 12-Aug | 26-Aug | 02-Sep | 09-Sep | Total | Average Score | Highest Score | Lowest Score | Played | Won | Lost |
|---|---|---|---|---|---|---|---|---|---|---|---|---|---|---|---|---|---|---|---|---|---|---|---|---|---|
| Dot | 21 | 21 | 21 | 21 | 21 | 21 | 16 | 21 | 21 | 21 | 21 | 21 | 21 | 21 | 21 | 21 | 7 | 21 | 359 | 19.94 | 21 | 7 | 18 | 16 | 2 |
| Cathy | 21 | 21 | 21 | 21 | 21 | 21 | 21 | 21 | 13 | 21 | 21 | 21 | 21 | 21 | 21 | 21 | 21 | 9 | 358 | 19.89 | 21 | 9 | 18 | 16 | 2 |
| Barbara | 21 | 19 | 21 | 21 | 12 | 21 | 13 | 21 | 9 | 11 | 21 | 18 | 6 | 21 | 21 | 15 | 18 | 19 | 308 | 17.11 | 21 | 6 | 18 | 8 | 10 |
| Shirley | | 20 | 21 | 14 | 13 | 21 | 16 | 21 | 18 | 21 | 21 | | | 21 | 21 | 21 | 21 | 21 | 291 | 19.4 | 21 | 13 | 15 | 10 | 5 |
| Barbara | 21 | 21 | 21 | 21 | | | 13 | 21 | 18 | 21 | | | 18 | 18 | 21 | 21 | 21 | 18 | 274 | 19.57 | 21 | 13 | 14 | 9 | 5 |
| Ann | 10 | 21 | 8 | 21 | 5 | 21 | 10 | 21 | 18 | 21 | 6 | 19 | | | 21 | 17 | 21 | 9 | 249 | 15.56 | 21 | 5 | 16 | 7 | 9 |
| Emily | | 0 | 1 | | 21 | 21 | 20 | 9 | | 11 | | | 18 | 21 | 21 | 13 | 20 | 14 | 190 | 14.62 | 21 | 0 | 13 | 4 | 9 |
| Eva | 21 | 14 | 21 | 18 | 21 | | | 5 | | 10 | | 21 | 6 | 7 | | | 21 | 10 | 175 | 14.58 | 21 | 5 | 12 | 5 | 7 |
| Norma | 8 | | 13 | 15 | 2 | 21 | 21 | 17 | 9 | | 10 | | | 3 | 21 | | | 21 | 161 | 13.42 | 21 | 2 | 12 | 4 | 8 |
| Josie | 21 | 21 | 6 | | 7 | 12 | 4 | | 3 | | 12 | 7 | 21 | 5 | | 21 | 9 | 7 | 156 | 11.14 | 21 | 3 | 14 | 4 | 10 |
| Joan | 19 | | | 16 | 12 | 0 | | | 15 | 14 | 15 | 15 | 7 | 0 | 21 | 0 | | | 134 | 11.17 | 21 | 0 | 12 | 1 | 11 |
| Flo | 7 | 7 | | 8 | | 18 | 6 | 4 | | 17 | 12 | 12 | 5 | | | 1 | 6 | | 103 | 8.583 | 18 | 1 | 12 | 0 | 12 |
| Lin | | | | | | | | 4 | | | 9 | 4 | 15 | 12 | 14 | | | | 58 | 9.667 | 15 | 4 | 6 | 0 | 6 |

The procedure is the same for 'smallest to largest' (ascending order), except click 'Smallest to Largest' from the drop down menu.

# Formatting your Spreadsheet

To emphasise certain parts of your spreadsheet such as totals or headings you can apply borders and shading to cells or groups of cells.

## Cell Alignment

This helps to align your data inside your cells and make it easier to read. To do this highlight the cells you want to apply the alignment to, then select 'centre' from the alignment icons highlighted above. The top three align vertically in the cell, the bottom three align horizontally in the cell.

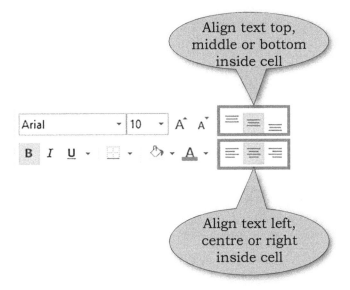

## Text Format

As well as aligning the text inside your cell, you can apply bold or italic effects to make certain parts such as headings stand out.

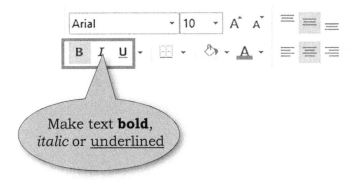

You can also change the font and size.

To do this in our spreadsheet highlight the headings ('22-Apr' to 'Fee Paid') and then click the bold icon highlighted below.

To align your text in the cells in the centre, select the cells you want then click the centre icon as highlighted below. *The top three icons align the text vertically, and the bottom three icons align the text horizontally.*

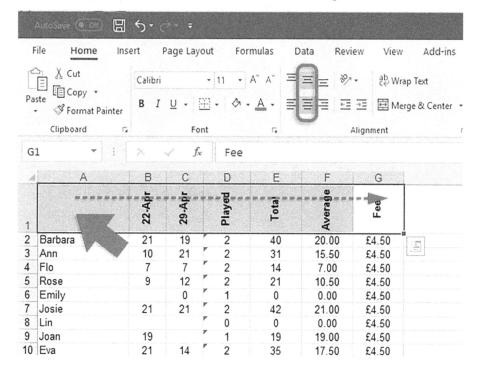

# Cell Borders

To apply borders to your spreadsheet, select with your mouse the cells you want to format. In this case, I am going to do the whole table. Right click on the selected cells and select 'format cells' from the menu.

I want the borders around all the cells both inside and the outline. So from the dialog box click 'outline' & 'inside'.

Now you can tweak the borders around the cells. It would make our spreadsheet easier to read if we divided the table into sections. Player name can be one section, scores can be the second section, total, average, and fee can be the third section. We can divide the table with a thicker line. First, highlight the total, average and fee paid columns, because this is one section. Right click, select 'format cells'.

| A | 22-Apr | 29-Apr | Played | Total | Average | Fee |
|---|---|---|---|---|---|---|
| Barbara | 21 | 19 | 2 | 40 | 20.00 | £ 4.50 |
| Ann | 10 | 21 | 2 | 31 | 15.50 | £ 4.50 |
| Flo | 7 | 7 | 2 | 14 | 7.00 | £ 4.50 |
| Rose | 9 | 12 | 2 | 21 | 10.50 | £ 4.50 |
| Emily | | 0 | 1 | 0 | 0.00 | £ 4.50 |
| Josie | 21 | 21 | 2 | 42 | 21.00 | £ 4.50 |
| Lin | | | 0 | 0 | 0.00 | £ 4.50 |
| Joan | 19 | | 1 | 19 | 19.00 | £ 4.50 |
| Eva | 21 | 14 | 2 | 35 | 17.50 | £ 4.50 |

From the dialog box, under the style section, select the size of your line, circled above in blue. Under the 'border section', select the left line and the right line, circled in red above, to apply the border to these edges.

Do this with the player names column too.

First, highlight the column as shown below. Right click on the grey selection and select 'format cells' from the menu...

From the 'style' section of the dialog box, select the style of line, eg dotted line, solid line, thick line etc. I'm going to click the thicker line in this example, circled above in blue.

Then from the 'border section', select the right line, circled in red above, to apply the border to the right edge of the selected column.

You can quickly apply borders using the borders icon on the home ribbon. This allows you to apply common border presets. Select your cells, then click the small down arrow next to the borders icon, indicated with the red arrow below, to reveal the drop down menu.

From the drop down menu select the border you want.

# Opening a New Sheet

Within your excel workbook, you can open more then one spreadsheet. To do this, click the '+' icon on the bottom left of your screen.

You'll see another blank tab appear along the bottom

Double click on the name of the sheet, 'sheet1' in this case, and enter a meaningful name.

# Copy Data Between Sheets

You can copy data between sheets using simple copy and paste. This works with simple data such as a name or number.

If you have formulas in the cells you want to copy, this poses more of a problem, as standard copy and paste will only copy the formula itself and you will get a "!REF" error. To get around this problem, you need to use the paste link feature.

To demonstrate this, I'm going to copy the list of names using standard copy and paste from one sheet to another. We're going to use the sample **Score Sheet Final.xlsx**.

First highlight the list of names.

| | A | B 22-Apr | C 29-Apr | D 06-May | E 13-May | F 20-May | G 27-May | H 03-Jun | I 10-Jun | J 17-Jun | K 24-Jun | L 01-Jul | M 08-Jul | N 15-Jul | O 29-Jul | P 12-Aug |
|---|---|---|---|---|---|---|---|---|---|---|---|---|---|---|---|---|
| 2 | Barbara | 21 | 19 | 21 | 21 | 12 | 21 | 13 | 21 | 9 | 11 | 21 | 18 | 6 | 21 | 21 |
| 3 | Ann | | 21 | 8 | 21 | 5 | 21 | 10 | 21 | 18 | 21 | 6 | 19 | | | 21 |
| 4 | Flo | | 7 | | 8 | | 18 | 6 | 4 | | 17 | 12 | 12 | 5 | | |
| 5 | Emily | | 0 | 1 | | 21 | 21 | 20 | 9 | | 11 | | | 18 | 21 | 21 |
| 6 | Barbara | 21 | 21 | 21 | 21 | | | 13 | 21 | 18 | 21 | | | 18 | 18 | 21 |
| 7 | Josie | 21 | 21 | 6 | | 7 | 12 | 4 | | 3 | | 12 | 7 | 21 | 5 | |
| 8 | Lin | | | | | | | | | 4 | | 9 | 4 | 15 | 12 | 14 |
| 9 | Joan | 19 | | | 16 | 12 | 0 | | | 15 | 14 | 15 | 15 | 7 | 0 | 21 |
| 10 | Eva | 21 | 14 | 21 | 18 | 21 | | | 5 | | 10 | | 21 | 6 | 7 | |
| 11 | Dot | 21 | 21 | 21 | 21 | 21 | 21 | 16 | 21 | 21 | 21 | 21 | 21 | 21 | 21 | 21 |
| 12 | Norma | 8 | | 13 | 15 | 2 | 21 | 21 | 17 | 9 | | 10 | | | 3 | 21 |
| 13 | Shirley | | 20 | 21 | 14 | 13 | 21 | 21 | 16 | 21 | 18 | 21 | 21 | | | 21 |
| 14 | Cathy | 21 | 21 | 21 | 21 | 21 | 21 | 21 | 21 | 13 | 21 | 21 | 21 | 21 | 21 | 21 |
| 15 | | | | | | | | | | | | | | | | |
| 16 | | | | | | | | | | | | | | | | |

From the home ribbon, select 'copy'.

Switch to the other sheet. Select the tab along the bottom of the screen.

Select cell A1 (where you want the names to appear).

Select 'paste' from the home ribbon.

Now, I want to add a second column to contain the total scores. I don't just want to copy the values, I want to copy the formulas, so the values update as the spreadsheet is updated.

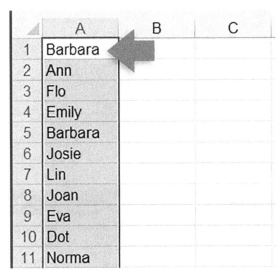

To do this, go back to the '2015' sheet, in the example workbook **Score Sheet Final.xlsx**.

Highlight the totals as shown below and select copy from the home ribbon.

| T2 | | | | fx | =SUM(B2:S2) | | | | | | | | | | | | | | | |

| | A | 22-Apr | 29-Apr | 06-May | 13-May | 20-May | 27-May | 03-Jun | 10-Jun | 17-Jun | 24-Jun | 01-Jul | 08-Jul | 15-Jul | 29-Jul | 12-Aug | 26-Aug | 02-Sep | 09-Sep | Total | Average Score |
|---|---|---|---|---|---|---|---|---|---|---|---|---|---|---|---|---|---|---|---|---|---|
| 2 | Barbara | 21 | 19 | 21 | 21 | 12 | 21 | 13 | 21 | 9 | 11 | 21 | 18 | 6 | 21 | 21 | 15 | 18 | 19 | 308 | 17.11 |
| 3 | Ann | 10 | 21 | 8 | 21 | 5 | 21 | 10 | 21 | 18 | 21 | 6 | 19 | | | 21 | 17 | 21 | 9 | 219 | 56 |
| 4 | Flo | 7 | 7 | | 8 | | 18 | 6 | 4 | | 17 | 12 | 12 | 5 | | | 1 | 6 | | 103 | 8.583 |
| 5 | Emily | | 0 | 1 | | 21 | 21 | 20 | 9 | | 11 | | 18 | 21 | 21 | 13 | 20 | 14 | | 190 | 14.62 |
| 6 | Barbara | 21 | 21 | 21 | 21 | | | 13 | 21 | 18 | 21 | | | 18 | 18 | 21 | 21 | 21 | 18 | 274 | 19.57 |
| 7 | Josie | 21 | 21 | 6 | | 7 | 12 | 4 | | 3 | | 12 | 7 | 21 | 5 | | 21 | 9 | 7 | 156 | 11.14 |
| 8 | Lin | | | | | | | | | 4 | | 9 | 4 | 15 | 12 | 14 | | | | 8 | 9.667 |
| 9 | Joan | 19 | | | 16 | 12 | 0 | | | 15 | 14 | 15 | 15 | 7 | 0 | 21 | 0 | | | 4 | 11.17 |
| 10 | Eva | 21 | 14 | 21 | 18 | 21 | | 5 | | 10 | | 21 | 6 | 7 | | | 21 | 10 | | 5 | 14.58 |
| 11 | Dot | 21 | 21 | 21 | 21 | 21 | 21 | 16 | 21 | 21 | 21 | 21 | 21 | 21 | 21 | 21 | 7 | 9 | | 9 | 19.94 |
| 12 | Norma | 8 | | 13 | 15 | 2 | 21 | 21 | 17 | 9 | | 10 | | 3 | 21 | | | 21 | | 151 | 13.42 |
| 13 | Shirley | | 20 | 21 | 14 | 13 | 21 | 21 | 16 | 21 | 18 | 21 | 21 | | | 21 | 21 | 21 | 21 | 291 | 19.4 |
| 14 | Cathy | 21 | 21 | 21 | 21 | 21 | 21 | 21 | 21 | 13 | 21 | 21 | 21 | 21 | 21 | 21 | 21 | 21 | 9 | 358 | 19.89 |

Switch to your other sheet: 'finals' and select the cell you want the values to start. In this case cell B1.

Click the down arrow under the 'paste' icon and select 'paste special'.

From bottom left of the dialog box select 'paste link'.

Operation
- ◉ None
- ○ Add
- ○ Subtract
- ○ Multiply
- ○ Divide

☐ Skip blanks          ☐ Transpose

[Paste Link]          [OK]          [Cancel]

# Freeze Panes

Large tables or long lists of data can often be difficult to read on a computer screen, sometimes scrolling down the list you can lose track of headings. To combat this, Excel has a feature that allows you to freeze a row or column, meaning the row/column will be on the screen at all times while you scroll down or across your screen. This is called 'freeze panes'.

If we have a look at our imported bank statement, **statement final.xls**, from the previous section, the list is quite long. Download and use the file **statement example.xls** if you haven't done the previous section.

It would be far easier to read if we froze the top row. To do this, go to your view ribbon and click 'freeze panes'. From the drop down menu, select 'freeze top row'. The top row of the list contains the headings.

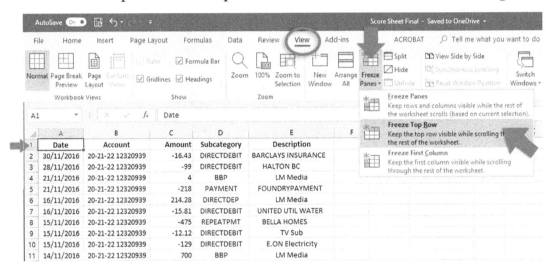

Now when you scroll down the list, the top row remains visible.

You can do the same with the first column. Click 'freeze first column' instead, from the drop down menu.

In the score sheet example, if I wanted the column with the player names as well as the dates to remain visible, you can do this with freeze panes.

I have included the file **score sheet final.xls** for you to practice with. You can download the file from

`www.elluminetpress.com/ms-excel`

When you click 'freeze panes' from the 'freeze panes' drop down menu, Excel will apply the freeze to the <u>rows above</u> and the <u>columns to the left</u> of the cell you have selected.

| | 22-Apr | 29-Apr | 06-May | 13-May | 20-May | 27-May | 03-Jun | 10-Jun | 17-Jun | 24-Jun | 01-Jul | 08-Jul |
|---|---|---|---|---|---|---|---|---|---|---|---|---|
| Barbara | 21 | 19 | 21 | 21 | 12 | 21 | 13 | 21 | 9 | 11 | 21 | 18 |
| Ann | 10 | 21 | 8 | 21 | 5 | 21 | 10 | 21 | 18 | 21 | 6 | 19 |
| Flo | 7 | 7 | | 8 | | | 18 | 6 | 4 | | 17 | 12 | 12 |
| Emily | | 0 | 1 | | 21 | 21 | 20 | 9 | | 11 | |
| Barbara | 21 | 21 | 21 | 21 | | | 13 | 21 | 18 | 21 | |
| Josie | 21 | 21 | 6 | | 7 | 12 | 4 | | 3 | | 12 | 7 |
| Lin | | | | | | | | | 4 | | 9 | 4 |
| Joan | 19 | | | 16 | 12 | 0 | | | 15 | 14 | 15 | 15 |

So in the example below, I have selected the cell B2 because I want to freeze the row above this cell (the dates), and freeze the column to the left of the cell (the names), as you can see in the screen print below.

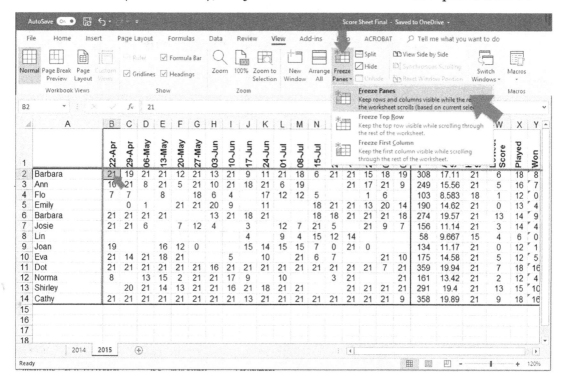

Once you have selected the cell. From your view ribbon, click 'freeze panes' then from the drop down menu click 'freeze panes'.

# Split Screen

This is particularly useful if you have a large spreadsheet where you need to see two different parts at the same time.

To split your screen vertically, select a cell in the top row where you want the screen to split. Go to your 'view' ribbon tab and select 'split'. A divider will appear.

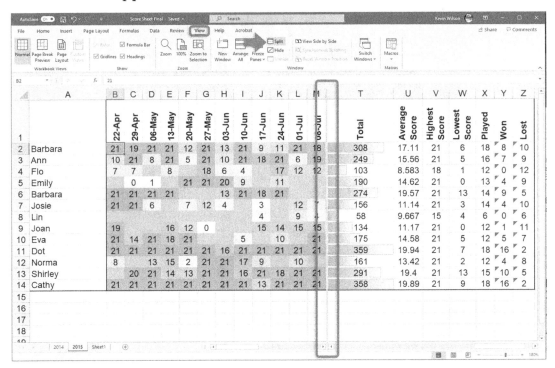

To split your screen horizontally, select a cell in the first column where you want the screen to split. Go to your 'view' ribbon tab and select 'split'. A divider will appear.

You can click and drag the divider to resize the split.

# Importing Data

You can import data into Excel. These could be lists of names and addresses or bank statement data you can download from your Bank. Make sure you download your data as comma separated, either a TXT file or CSV file.

You can import the data using Excel's import wizard. As an example, I have included some test data from a sample bank statement for you to practice with.

You can download the test data file **statement test data.csv** from

`www.elluminetpress.com/ms-excel`

To import the data, open a new spreadsheet and from the data ribbon, click 'From Text/CSV'.

In the dialog box that appears, select your data file. In this example **statement test data.csv**.

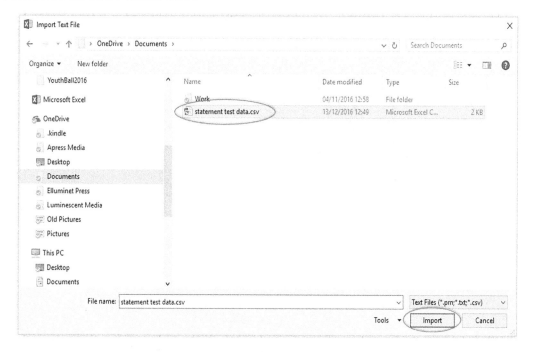

When you have done that, click import.

Now you have to tell Excel how your data is 'delimited' or separated from each other. To show you what this means, if we open the file in notepad, you can see we have a list of transactions. The data in each transaction in the list is separated or 'delimited' with a comma: Date, Account Number, Amount, Sub Category, Description.

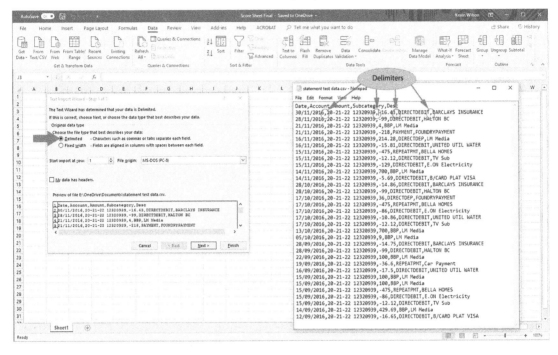

So in the dialog box, select 'delimited' and click next.

The data is separated, or delimited by a comma. So in the 'delimiters' section, uncheck 'tab' and click the check box next to 'comma'.

Notice the data in the preview has now been separated into Excel columns. Click 'finish'.

Select the first cell where you want to insert the data. Cell A1 is usually a good start on a blank sheet.

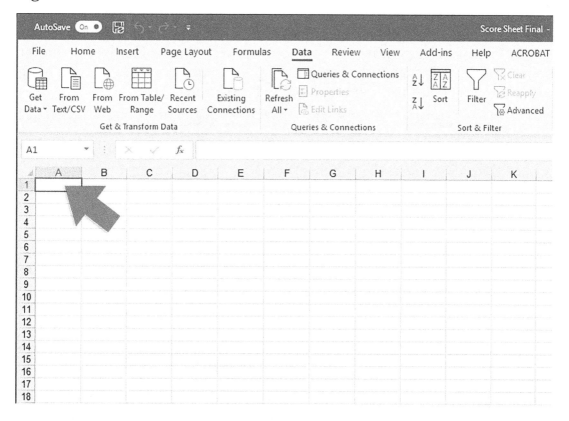

If you want the data to be imported into a new worksheet, just click the radio button next to 'new worksheet' at the bottom of the dialog box.

Click OK when you're done.

Save your spreadsheet as **statement final.xls**

# Conditional Formatting

Conditional formatting allows you to change the format of a cell depending on the cell's contents or value. For example, in our score sheet, I want to highlight all the wins for each player. In this particular sport a score of 21 is a win, so we can apply some conditional formatting to change the colour of each cell with the number 21.

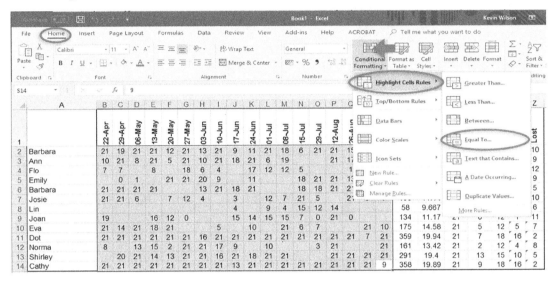

First, highlight the range of cells you want to apply the conditional formatting to. In this example, it's the range B2 to S14 - all the player's scores.

Next, from your home ribbon, click 'conditional formatting'. You'll see a drop down menu with some options. We want to highlight the cells that have a score of 21, so in the menu, go to 'highlight cell rules'. From the slide out, you can select your conditions. In this example, we're highlighting cells with a value equal to 21, so click 'equal to...'

In the 'equal to' dialog box, enter the number your cells must be equal to, in this example, '21'. In the drop down box, select a format. Green is usually good to indicate positives like a win, so select 'green fill with dark green text'. Click OK when you're done.

Taking it a step further, you can also apply different pre-set effects to the cells according to their value. For example, in our scoring sheet, you could have a different shade for each value. 21 being the highest score and a win could be dark green, and each value below 21 could have a lighter shade as the number decreases. So you end up with a very light green at the lowest scores.

You can do this with colour scales. From your home ribbon, click 'conditional formatting', select 'colour scales', then from the slide out menu, select a style. I'm going to go for the bottom left option with a dark to green colour scale.

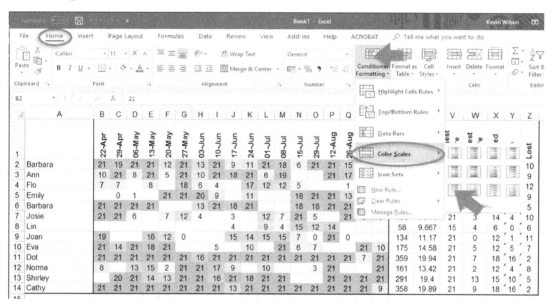

Any blank cells in the table are when a player was either absent or didn't play. We could highlight these in light red. For this one, select 'conditional formatting' from your home ribbon, go to 'highlight cell rules' and from the slide out menu, click 'more rules'.

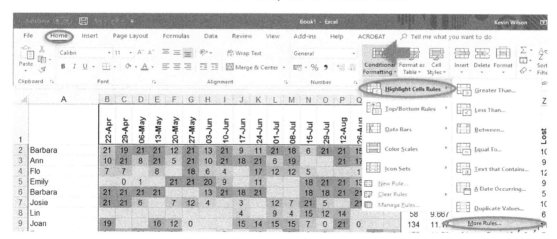

From the dialog box, in the 'select a rule type' section, select 'format only cells that contain', because we are formatting according to a specific value or condition (ie blank cells).

Then in the 'edit the rule description' section, change this to 'blanks' because we are checking for blank cells.

Next click 'format', then select a colour to shade the cell when Excel finds a blank. In this example, I'm choosing a light red.

Click 'ok' on both dialog boxes.

For the totals column you could add data bars. You'll need to widen the totals column a bit to see the effect.

Select the total column, from your home ribbon click 'conditional formatting'.

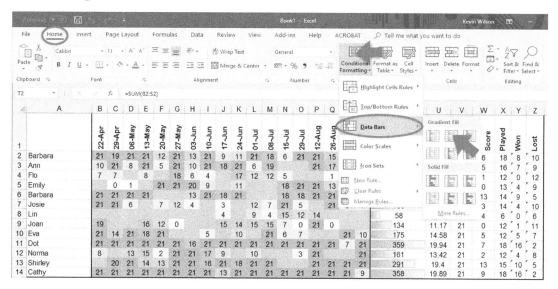

Go down to 'data bars' and select a gradient fill from the slide out menu.

You should end up with something like this. As you can see the higher the final score, the longer the data bar. This is useful for making totals at a glance easier to process.

| | 22-Apr | 29-Apr | 06-May | 13-May | 20-May | 27-May | 03-Jun | 10-Jun | 17-Jun | 24-Jun | 01-Jul | 08-Jul | 15-Jul | 29-Jul | 12-Aug | 26-Aug | 02-Sep | 09-Sep | Total |
|---|---|---|---|---|---|---|---|---|---|---|---|---|---|---|---|---|---|---|---|
| Barbara | 21 | 19 | 21 | 21 | 12 | 21 | 13 | 21 | 9 | 11 | 21 | 18 | 6 | 21 | 21 | 15 | 18 | 19 | 308 |
| Ann | 10 | 21 | 8 | 21 | 5 | 21 | 10 | 21 | 18 | 21 | 6 | 19 | | | 21 | 17 | 21 | 9 | 249 |
| Flo | 7 | 7 | | 8 | | 18 | 6 | 4 | | 17 | 12 | 12 | 5 | | | 1 | 6 | | 103 |
| Emily | | 0 | 1 | | 21 | 21 | 20 | 9 | | 11 | | 18 | 21 | 21 | 13 | 20 | 14 | | 190 |
| Barbara | 21 | 21 | 21 | 21 | | | 13 | 21 | 18 | 21 | | 18 | 18 | 21 | 21 | 21 | 18 | | 274 |
| Josie | 21 | 21 | 6 | | 7 | 12 | 4 | | 3 | | 12 | 7 | 21 | 5 | | 21 | 9 | 7 | 156 |
| Lin | | | | | | | | 4 | | 9 | 4 | 15 | 12 | 14 | | | | | 58 |
| Joan | 19 | | | 16 | 12 | 0 | | 15 | 14 | 15 | 15 | 7 | 0 | 21 | 0 | | | | 134 |
| Eva | 21 | 14 | 21 | 18 | 21 | | | 5 | | 10 | | 21 | 6 | 7 | | 21 | 10 | | 175 |
| Dot | 21 | 21 | 21 | 21 | 21 | 21 | 16 | 21 | 21 | 21 | 21 | 21 | 21 | 21 | 21 | 21 | 7 | 21 | 359 |
| Norma | 8 | | 13 | 15 | 2 | 21 | 21 | 17 | 9 | | 10 | | | 3 | 21 | | | 21 | 161 |
| Shirley | | 20 | 21 | 14 | 13 | 21 | 21 | 16 | 21 | 18 | 21 | 21 | | | 21 | 21 | 21 | 21 | 291 |
| Cathy | 21 | 21 | 21 | 21 | 21 | 21 | 21 | 21 | 13 | 21 | 21 | 21 | 21 | 21 | 21 | 21 | 21 | 9 | 358 |

# Managing Workbooks

In this section, we'll take a look at printing spreadsheets, working with workbooks, page setup, as well as saving your work and exporting as a different format.

Before we begin, throughout this section, we will be using the resource files.

You can download these files from

`www.elluminetpress.com/ms-excel`

Go down to the files section and click the icons to download the documents to the documents folder on your PC.

# Using Multiple Workbooks

If you have multiple workbooks open at a time, you can easily switch between them on Windows 10. To do this, click the Word icon, on your taskbar.

The workbooks that are currently open will show up as thumbnails. Just click one of the thumbnails to switch to that document.

You can also display the workbooks side by side. Go to your view ribbon and click 'side by side'

Turn off the synchronous scrolling, otherwise both sheets will scroll at the same time, although this feature can be useful if you are comparing two workbooks.

# Chapter 4: Managing Workbooks

You can also arrange the windows vertically if that's easier to read. Go to your view ribbon, click 'arrange all'.

From the pop up dialog box select 'vertical'.

All files open in Excel will be arranged on your screen according to the setting you chose. In this case the two open windows are arranged vertically.

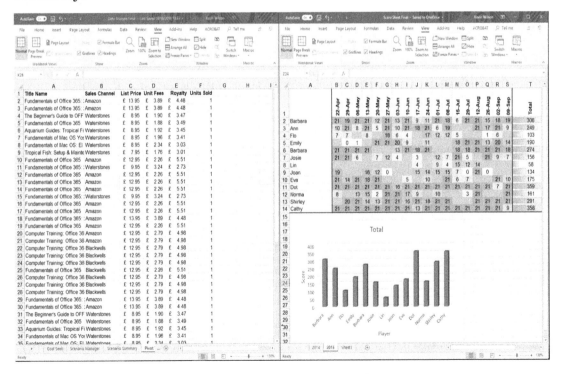

# Printing your Spreadsheet

To print your document, click 'file' on the top left hand corner of the screen

From the menu on the left hand side of the screen, select print.

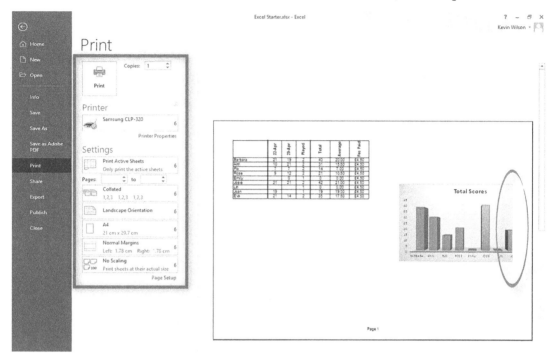

From the settings shown above, you can select the number of copies, the printer you're using, the range of pages you want to print. For example, if you just want to print the first page, last page etc.

You can select landscape or portrait paper orientation - use landscape for printing most spreadsheets.

Select paper size such as letter, legal, A3 or A4.

Margins, you can adjust from here. Select normal, wide margins or narrow margins.

Scaling can be used to make the spreadsheet bigger or smaller to fit your page.

When printing in Excel, keep an eye on the preview on the right hand side of the screen above. Notice how the chart is cut off. Sometimes columns can be cut off too. You can adjust this by going back to your spreadsheet- clicking the back arrow on the very top left of the screen. This will take you back to your spreadsheet.

Excel will have placed dotted lines showing the edge of the page print area. Move the content you want on the page inside this area, either by moving charts by dragging or resizing columns etc.

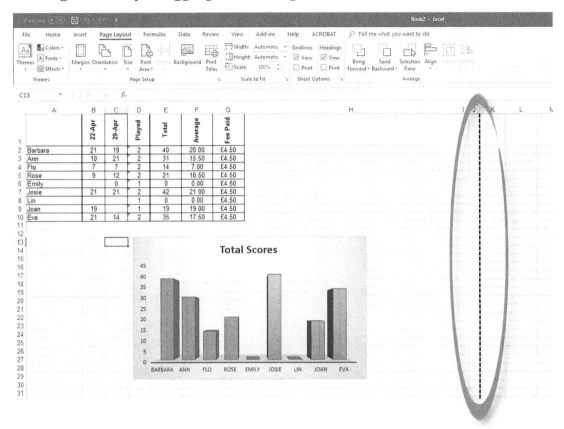

Also check your margins on the page layout ribbon, select narrow.

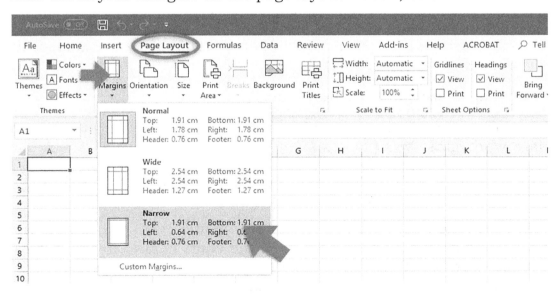

Now go to print your spreadsheet as before. (File -> Print).

Once you are happy with the print preview, print your document.

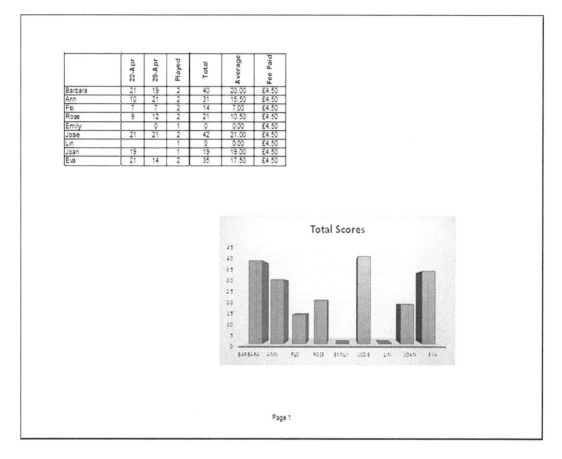

| | 22-Apr | 29-Apr | Played | Total | Average | Fee Paid |
|---|---|---|---|---|---|---|
| Barbara | 21 | 19 | 2 | 40 | 20.00 | £4.50 |
| Ann | 10 | 21 | 2 | 31 | 15.50 | £4.50 |
| Flo | 7 | 7 | 2 | 14 | 7.00 | £4.50 |
| Rose | 9 | 12 | 2 | 21 | 10.50 | £4.50 |
| Emily | | | 0 | 1 | 0 | 0.00 | £4.50 |
| Josie | 21 | 21 | 2 | 42 | 21.00 | £4.50 |
| Lin | | | 1 | 0 | 0.00 | £4.50 |
| Joan | 19 | | 1 | 19 | 19.00 | £4.50 |
| Eva | 21 | 14 | 2 | 35 | 17.50 | £4.50 |

Click the print icon to send the spreadsheet to the printer.

# Print

Copies: 1

Print

## Printer

Samsung CLP-320                    6

Printer Properties

You can make more detailed changes using the 'page setup' settings, in the following sections.

67-12-22.

# Page Setup

You can use page setup to change how your spreadsheet is displayed on a printed page.

To open the page setup options, click file. Then from the backstage that appears, click 'print'.

You'll see some basic settings listed down the left of the print window. These are usually the most used settings for changing number of copies printed, single sided or double sided print, orientation - landscape or portrait, paper size - legal or A4, margins and scaling - useful if your spreadsheet just doesn't fit on a page.

To open the full page setup options, click 'page setup' at the bottom of the screen, circled above.

You'll see a dialog box appear with four tabs across the top: page, margins, header/footer and sheet.

# Page Options

From the page tab you can set page orientation to portrait or landscape.

Underneath, you have some options for scaling your spreadsheet. This is useful if you want to shrink your spreadsheet down to fit onto one page. Do this by adjusting the size percentage in the 'adjust to...' field.

If you have quite a large spreadsheet that wont fit on one page, you can scale the spreadsheet across multiple pages. If we look at our example **Score Sheet Final.xlsx** on '2014' worksheet, you'll see that the sheet and the charts appear across 5 pages.

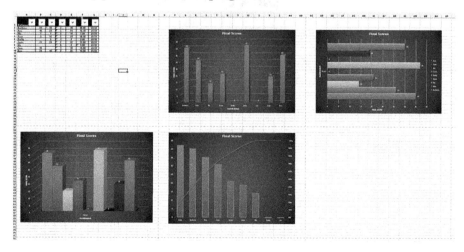

In the scaling section of the page tab, click fit to, then make sure it's set to **1** page wide by **1** page tall.

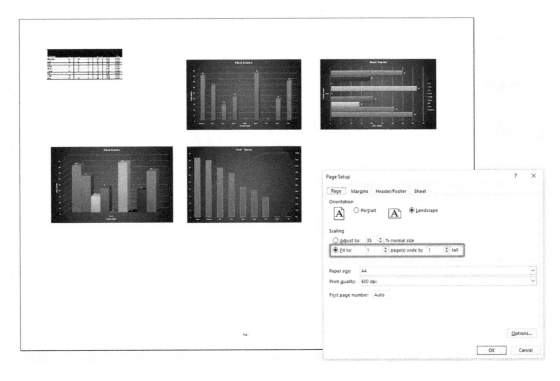

This will fit the spreadsheet to one page.

You can also use the shortcuts on the print screen settings section, as indicated below.

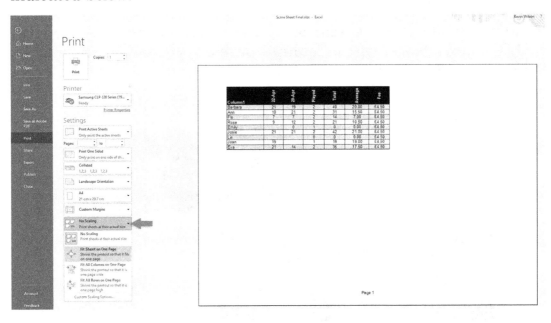

Click 'fit sheet on one page'.

# Margins

The margin is the space between the data and the edge of the printed page.

In the illustration below, the top margins are shown in red, the left and right margins are shown in blue and the header/footer margins are shown in green.

To adjust your margins, go to your page layout ribbon and click 'margins'. From the drop down menu, you can select some presets.

Wide margins give your more space around the edges of your document but you can fit less data on your page.

Narrow margins reduce the space around the edges and allows you to squeeze more onto your page - useful if your spreadsheet just doesn't fit on your page.

# Customising Margins

You can customise your margins to your own specifications. A quick way to do this is to click file, then from the backstage click 'print'.

From the print preview screen, click the 'show margins' icon located on the bottom right of your screen.

You'll see the margin lines appear on the preview. Click and drag the lines to adjust the margins.

# Headers & Footers

Headers and footers appear at the top and bottom of your spreadsheet when it is printed out. You won't see any headers and footers when building your spreadsheet, unless you are in page layout mode.

To quickly edit your headers & footers, click on the 'page layout' icon on the bottom right of your screen. You'll see your spreadsheet on screen divide up into printable pages.

Along the top and bottom, you'll see place holders for your headers & footers. There are three boxes. Click in each of these to add headings.

The left box is to add text to the left hand side, the centre box for centred text and the right hand box for right aligned text.

To add a header, click in one of these boxes. In this example, I am using the file **score sheet final.xlsx**. I am going to add the date to the left box, the title in the centre box and my initials to the right hand box.

Click in the left hand header box. When you click in one of these boxes, you'll notice a new ribbon appears called 'design'. This ribbon contains all your header and footer tools.

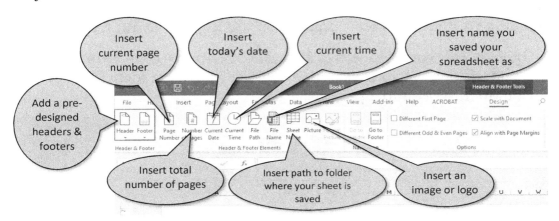

From the design ribbon click 'current date'. This will add today's date to the header box.

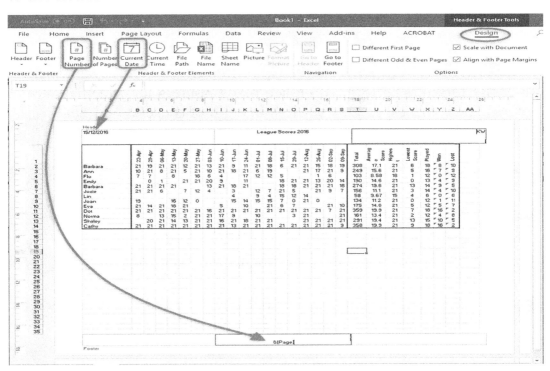

Click the centre box and type 'League Scores 2019' and in the right hand box type your initials. If you want to change the font or text size, you can do this from your home ribbon as normal.

To go to the footer, click in the footer section at the bottom of the page preview. Click the centre box, then from the design ribbon click 'page number.

# Page Print Order

Click file, then select print from the backstage. Click 'page setup'. Select the 'sheet' tab.

If we take a look at the page order section, this tells Excel in what order to print your spreadsheet if it's larger than one printed page. To explain what this means, if we come out of print preview and take a look at our spreadsheet, you'll notice that Excel has put in some dotted lines.

These lines are where Excel has divided your spreadsheet into pages according to your page size and orientation.

Lets have a look at an example with some data. Open **Score Sheet Final.xlsx** and open the '2014' worksheet.

If you select 'down then over' from the sheet tab on the page setup dialog box, your spreadsheet will print out in this order

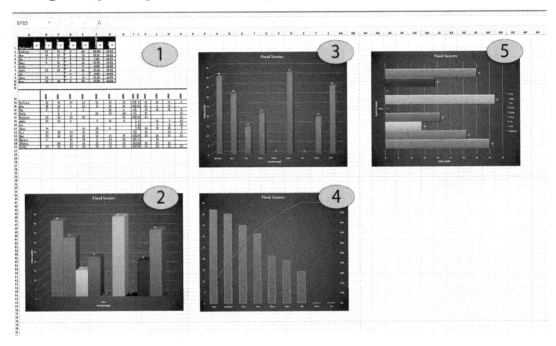

If you select 'over then down', your spreadsheet will print out like this

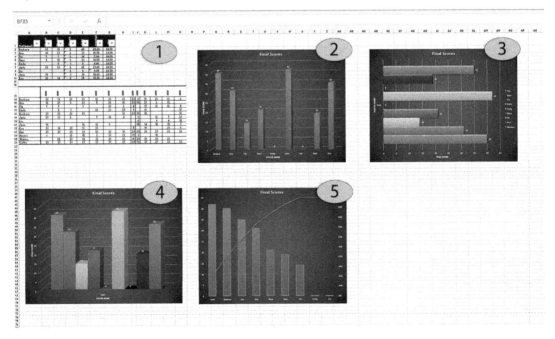

Notice the order pages are printed out.

# Print Options

Click file, then select print from the backstage. Click 'page setup'. Select the 'sheet' tab.

## Print Row and Column Headers

This prints the row and column reference headers, circled below. Excel doesn't print these by default but should you need to include them in a printout, you can turn them on from the sheet tab.

From the sheet tab in the page setup dialog box, go down to the print section and select 'row and column headings'.

Click OK when you're done. Notice the column and row reference headers are visible in the print preview, shown above.

# Print Gridlines

This feature prints the gridlines on your spreadsheets regardless if you have added borders when formatting your sheet.

Excel doesn't print these by default but should you need to include them in a printout, you can turn them on from the sheet tab. This feature can be useful for making data clearer in a printout.

From the sheet tab in the page setup dialog box, go down to the print section and select 'gridlines'.

Click OK when you're done. Notice the gridlines are visible in the print preview as well as the border's we added when formatting our spreadsheet, as shown above.

# Print Selection

Print selection allows you to select a specific part of your spreadsheet to print out. You do this by setting a print area.

To set a print area, highlight the area you want to print. In the example **Score Sheet Final.xlsx**, I want to print out the scores and the total, which is the first half of the score table. So highlight A1 to T14, as shown below.

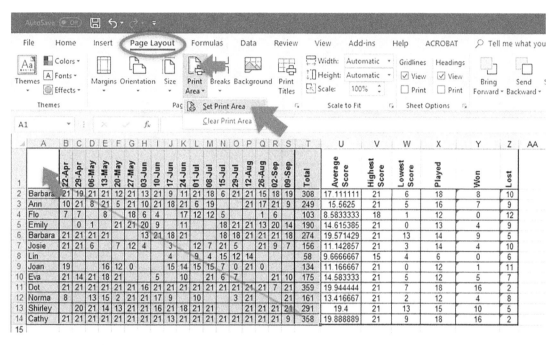

Go to your page layout ribbon and select 'print area'. From the drop down menu, click 'set print area'.

This will tell Excel that you only want to include this area in your printout.

# Print Titles

If we take a look at our example bank statement **Statement Example. xlsx,** you'll notice when you go to print preview, it prints out over two pages. If you look at the second page, you'll see Excel has not printed the headings.

You can mark rows and columns you want to appear on each page using the print titles feature. To do this, go to your page layout ribbon and click 'print titles'.

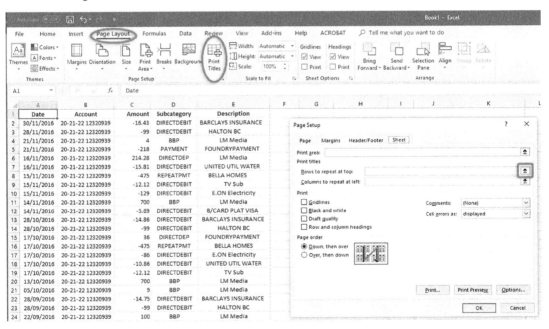

From the dialog box click the small arrow next to 'rows to repeat at top'. We want to repeat the top row on all pages - the column titles.

Now select the top row of the spreadsheet, then click the X on the top right of the small dialog box.

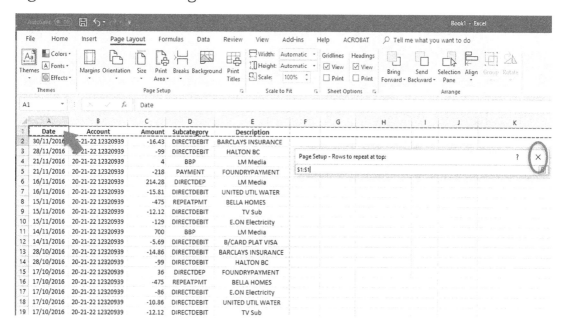

Click OK on dialog box that appears.

Now, when you go to print preview, you'll see that the top row appears on every page. You can do this with columns too, just select 'columns to repeat at left' from the dialog box instead of 'rows to repeat at top'.

# Show & Print Formulas

Sometimes it's useful to be able to view the formulas themselves instead of the result. This helps proof reading and checking to make sure formulas are correct.

To show the formulas, go to your formulas ribbon and click 'show formulas'. To see the whole formula, you might have to adjust the width of the columns.

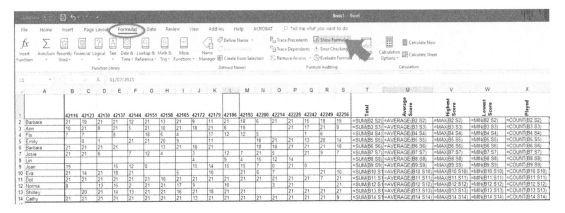

You can also print these formulas if you need to in the normal way. Click file then print.

When you print these formulas, you might need to do some scaling to make them fit onto one page. Use the scaling options at the bottom of the print preview window.

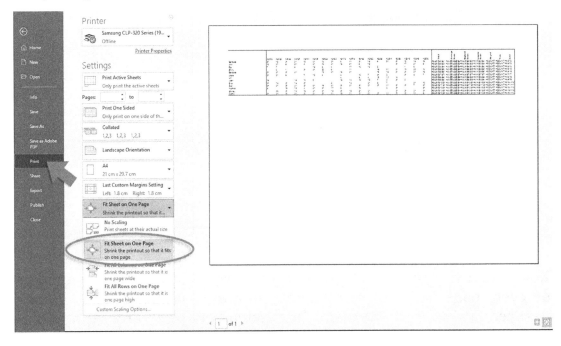

# Opening a Saved Workbook

If Excel is already open you can open previously saved workbooks by clicking the FILE menu on the top left of your screen.

From the green bar along the left hand side click 'open', click 'OneDrive - Personal'.

From the list, select the workbook you want to open. The workbook from a previous project was saved as 'excel final.xlsx', so this is the one I am going to open here. Double click the file name to open it.

For convenience, instead of searching through your OneDrive, Excel lists all your most recently opened Excel files. You can view these by selecting 'recent'. Selecting 'workbooks' shows your recently opened spreadsheets, 'folders' shows the folders of the spreadsheets recently opened

Your latest files will be listed first.

Double click the file name to open it.

# Saving Workbooks

To save files, click the small disk icon in the top left hand corner of your screen.

Excel also has an auto save option. This means Excel will automatically save your workbook each time you make a change. To turn this feature on or off, click the 'autosave' icon.

Select your OneDrive - Personal, then select a folder you want to save the file into, eg 'documents'.

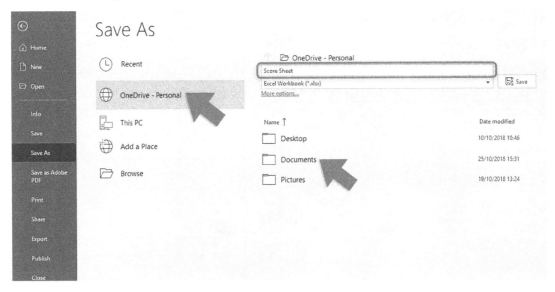

Enter a meaningful name in the text field indicated above by the red arrow.

Click save.

# Save as a Different Format

You can save your Excel spreadsheets in different formats depending on what you want to do with the file. You can save as CSV, web pages, and PDFs.

To save files in a different format, eg PDF, click 'file'.

From the backstage, click 'save' or 'save a copy'. Then select OneDrive.

Select where you want to save the file.

Give the file a meaningful name.

Underneath, select the small down arrow next to the file type field. From the drop down menu, select the file format you want to use.

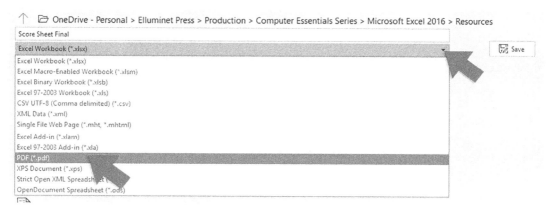

Click 'save' when you're done.

# Formulas & Functions

In this section, we'll take a look at creating formulas to manipulate data and basic functions.

Before we begin, throughout this section, we will be using the resource files.

You can download these files from

`www.elluminetpress.com/ms-excel`

Go down to the files section and click the icons to download the documents to the documents folder on your PC.

# Using Formulas

If I wanted to add up all the scores in my score sheet, I could add another column called total and enter a formula to add up the scores for the two weeks the player has played.

To do this, I need to find the cell references for Barbara's scores.

Her scores are in row 2 and columns B and C circled below.

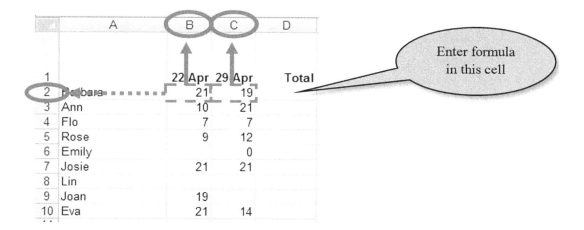

So the cell references are B2 for her score of 21, and C2 for her score of 19.

So we enter into the cell under the heading 'total'

    = B2+C2

Remember all formulas must start with an equals sign (**=**).

To save you entering the formula for each row, you can replicate it instead.

If you click on the cell D2, where you entered the formula above, you will notice on the bottom right of the box, a small square handle.

I've enlarged the image so you can see it clearly.

Drag this handle down the rest of the column. You can also double click this handle to fill the rest of the column automatically.

| D2 | ▼ | ⋮ | ✕ | ✓ | *fx* | =C2+B2 |

| | A | B 22-Apr | C 29-Apr | D Total |
|---|---|---|---|---|
| 1 | | | | |
| 2 | Barbara | 21 | 19 | 40 |
| 3 | Ann | 10 | 21 | |
| 4 | Flo | 7 | 7 | |
| 5 | Rose | 9 | 12 | |
| 6 | Emily | | 0 | |
| 7 | Josie | 21 | 21 | |
| 8 | Lin | | | |
| 9 | Joan | 19 | | |
| 10 | Eva | 21 | 14 | |
| 11 | | | | |

Excel will automatically copy the formula and calculate the rest of the totals for you, without you having to enter the formulas for each row.

# BIDMAS Rule

BIDMAS (sometimes BODMAS) is an acronym commonly used to remember mathematical operator priority.

**B**rackets ( )
**I**ndices (square roots: $\sqrt{}$, exponents: squared$^2$ or cubed$^3$)
**D**ivide /
**M**ultiply *
**A**dd +
**S**ubtract -

For example, if you wanted to add 20% sales tax to a price of £12.95, you could do something like this...

$$Total = 12.95 + \left(12.95 * \frac{20}{100}\right)$$

Do the bit circled in red first [multiply & divide], then the addition.

# Using Functions

A function is a pre-defined formula. Excel has hundreds of different functions all designed to make analysing your data easier. You can find most of these functions on the formulas ribbon.

The functions are sorted into groups in the 'function library' section. Just click on these to view the list of functions.

To insert a function into a cell, use the formula bar just under the ribbon menu. So, if I wanted to add a function to cell A1, select A1, then either type the function into the text field or click the 'fx' icon.

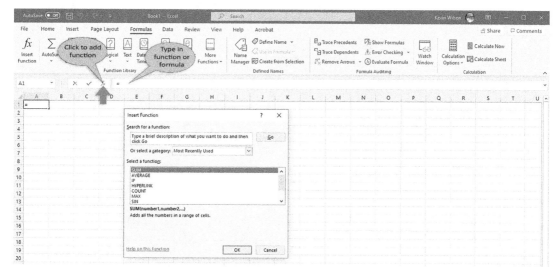

If you click the 'fx' icon, select your function from the dialog box.

# Count

Say I wanted to count the number of games played automatically. I could do this with a function.

Insert a new column after "29 Apr" into the spreadsheet and call it "Played". To do this, right click on the D column (the 'Total' column) and from the menu click insert.

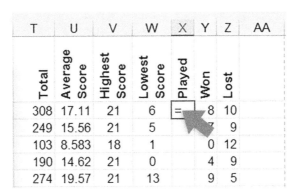

Make sure you have selected the cell you want the formula to appear in, then click 'insert function' (*fx*).

In the insert function dialog box, select the count function from the list then click OK. Type it into the 'search for a function' field if it isn't listed.

Now we need to tell the count function what we want it to count. We want to count the number of games played.

Barbara's scores are in cells B2:S2, so highlight these by dragging your mouse over them, as shown below

| | A | 22-Apr | 29-Apr | 06-May | 13-May | 20-May | 27-May | 03-Jun | 10-Jun | 17-Jun | 24-Jun | 01-Jul | 08-Jul | 15-Jul | 29-Jul | 12-Aug | 26-Aug | 02-Sep | 09-Sep | Total | Average Score | Highest Score |
|---|---|---|---|---|---|---|---|---|---|---|---|---|---|---|---|---|---|---|---|---|---|---|
| 1 | | | | | | | | | | | | | | | | | | | | | | |
| 2 | Barbara | 21 | 19 | 21 | 21 | 12 | 21 | 13 | 21 | 9 | 11 | 21 | 18 | 6 | 21 | 21 | 15 | 18 | 19 | 308 | 17.11 | 21 |
| 3 | Ann | 10 | 21 | 8 | 21 | 5 | 21 | 10 | 21 | 18 | 21 | 6 | 19 | | | 21 | 17 | 21 | 9 | 249 | 15.56 | 21 |

Click OK in the dialog box.

You can see she has played 18 games. Now we can replicate the formula as we did before. Click and drag the small square handle on the bottom right hand side of the cell.

| Played | Won | Lost |
|---|---|---|
| 18 | 8 | 10 |
| | 7 | 9 |
| | 0 | 12 |
| | 4 | 9 |
| | 9 | 5 |
| | 4 | 10 |

Drag it down to fill the rest of the column.

# CountIf

Counting the number of wins gets a little bit more tricky. In this particular sport, a win is the first to 21 points. So we can count the '21s' in the players' scores.

To do this, we use the 'CountIf' function. This function counts a value depending on a certain condition, in this case if the value is 21 or not.

I have inserted another column called 'won'. Click in the first cell of that column. This is where we want the result to appear.

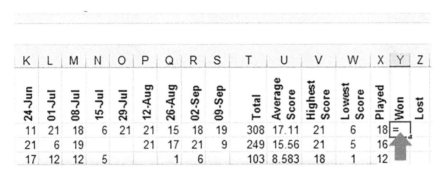

To insert a CountIf function, click the insert function icon on your ribbon (*fx*).

From the dialog box that appears, select 'CountIf'. If it isn't listed, type countif into the search field. Click OK.

Select the range of values you want to count. For Barbara's scores, the range is B2:S2. To do this, click on the cell B2 and drag your mouse over to S2.

In the criteria field enter the number 21, because we want to count the number of '21s' in the range.

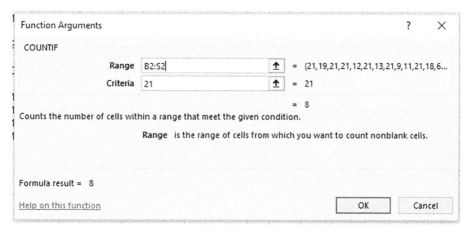

Click OK.

Now replicate the function down the rest of the column. Drag the square handle on the bottom right of the cell.

# Auto Sum

Auto sum, as its name suggests, adds up all the values in a row or column.

To add up a row, click on the cell you want the total to appear in. In this example, I have created a column for totals, and I want the total for the first player to appear in cell T2, circled below in the illustration.

Next, add the auto sum function. You'll find this on your home ribbon. Click on the 'auto sum' icon.

You'll notice, the auto sum function has highlighted the row I want to add up. Press the enter key on your keyboard to execute the function.

Now replicate the function to fill the rest of the column by dragging the handle down, as shown below.

| | E | F | G | H | I | J | K | L | M | N | O | P | Q | R | S | T | U | V | W | X |
|---|---|---|---|---|---|---|---|---|---|---|---|---|---|---|---|---|---|---|---|---|
| 1 | 13-May | 20-May | 27-May | 03-Jun | 10-Jun | 17-Jun | 24-Jun | 01-Jul | 08-Jul | 15-Jul | 29-Jul | 12-Aug | 26-Aug | 02-Sep | 09-Sep | Total | Played | Won | Lost | |
| 2 | 21 | 12 | 21 | 13 | 21 | 9 | 11 | 21 | 18 | 6 | 21 | 21 | 15 | 18 | 19 | 308 | 18 | 8 | 10 | |
| 3 | 21 | 5 | 21 | 10 | 21 | 18 | 21 | 6 | 19 | | | 21 | 17 | 21 | 9 | | 16 | 7 | 9 | |
| 4 | 8 | | 18 | 6 | 4 | | 17 | 12 | 12 | 5 | | | 1 | 6 | | | 12 | | 12 | |
| 5 | | 21 | 21 | 20 | 9 | | 11 | | | 18 | 21 | 21 | 13 | 20 | 14 | | 13 | 4 | 9 | |
| 6 | 21 | | | 13 | 21 | 18 | 21 | | | 18 | 18 | 21 | 21 | 21 | 18 | | 14 | 9 | 5 | |
| 7 | | 7 | 12 | 4 | | 3 | | 12 | 7 | 21 | 5 | | 21 | 9 | 7 | | 14 | 4 | 10 | |
| 8 | | | | 4 | | | 9 | 4 | 15 | 12 | 14 | | | | | | 6 | | 6 | |
| 9 | 16 | 12 | 0 | | 15 | 14 | 15 | 15 | 7 | 0 | 21 | 0 | | | | | 12 | 1 | 11 | |

# Average

Average finds the middle number in a row or column. To find the average, click on the cell you want the result to appear in. In this example, I have inserted a column for average score, and I want the average for the first player to appear in cell U2, circled below left in the illustration.

Next, add the average function. You'll find this on your home ribbon. Click on the small down arrow next to the auto sum icon. From the drop down menu, select 'average'. Now, you'll notice that the average function includes the totals column. This is not what we want to average, so you'll need to select the range B2:S2. Click on the cell B2 and drag the box across to S2. Hit return to enter the function.

Now replicate the function down the rest of the column.

| 08 | 15 | 29 | 12 | 26 | 02 | 09 | Tc | Av Sc | Pl | W | Lc |
|----|----|----|----|----|----|----|-----|-------|----|---|----|
| 18 | 6 | 21 | 21 | 15 | 18 | 19 | 308 | 17.1 | 18 | 8 | 10 |
| 19 | | | 21 | 17 | 21 | 9 | 249 | 15.6 | 16 | 7 | 9 |
| 12 | 5 | | | 1 | 6 | | 103 | 8.58 | 12 | | 12 |
| | | 18 | 21 | 21 | 13 | 20 | 14 | 190 | 14.6 | 13 | 4 | 9 |
| | | 18 | 18 | 21 | 21 | 21 | 18 | 274 | 19.6 | 14 | 9 | 5 |
| 7 | 21 | 5 | | 21 | 9 | 7 | 156 | 11.1 | 14 | 4 | 10 |

# Max & Min

Max returns the largest number in a selected range of values, and min returns the smallest number.

Select the cell you want the result to appear in. I have added two new columns, one for highest score and one for lowest score. I'm going to use the max function in the 'highest score' column.

From your home ribbon, click the small down arrow next to the auto sum icon, and from the drop down menu, select 'max'.

Now, you'll notice that the max function has included 'total' and 'average score', this is not what we want. Select the range B2:S2 - click on the cell B2, then drag your mouse pointer over to S2.

Hit enter to execute the function, then drag the square handle on the bottom right of the cell to replicate the function down the rest of the column.

| Total | Average Score | Highest Score | Lowest Score |
|---|---|---|---|
| 308 | 17.1 | 21 | |
| 249 | 15.6 | | |
| 103 | 8.58 | | |
| 190 | 14.6 | | |

The procedure is exactly the same for the Min function, except from the auto sum drop down menu select 'min' instead of 'max'. Give it a try.

# IF Function

If functions are called conditional functions and test whether a condition is true or false. The function returns a different result for the true condition and another result for false.

```
= (IF condition, result-if-true, result-if-false)
```

Can be read as

```
If test condition is true,
     execute result-if-true
else
     execute result-if-false
```

In the example **IF function demo.xlsx**, we are going to apply a conditional function to calculate our shipping cost. The rule is, free delivery for orders over £25, otherwise a shipping charge of £3.99 applies.

To insert an IF function, click on the cell you want the calculation to appear in (D12).

Then go to your formulas ribbon and click 'insert function'.

From the dialog box that appears, select IF. *If the function isn't in the list, type IF into the search field and click 'go'.*

Click OK when you're done.

Now to build the IF function. First, we need to find out if the total is greater than or equal to 25.

In the function arguments dialog box, click in the 'logical test' field

The net total is in cell D11, so click D11 to add this cell to the logical test.

Click back in the logical test field and add the following:

>=25

In the 'value if true' field type 0, because if the net total is over 25, the logical test condition is true, so it's free delivery over £25

In the 'value if false' type 3.99, because if it's under £25 we charge the fee.

Click OK.

Because the net total is £27.46, this is over 25, so the shipping is 0.

Try adjusting the number of items and see what happens when the total goes below £25.

# VLookup

VLOOKUP searches for a value in the first column of a specified table, and returns a value from the specified adjacent column.

```
=VLOOKUP (value to look for,
          table to retrieve value from,
               column number with value to return,
                    true for exact/false for approx)
```

In the example **VLOOKUP function demo.xlsx**, we are going to apply a lookup function to calculate our shipping cost according to the shipping rates table (F15:G20).

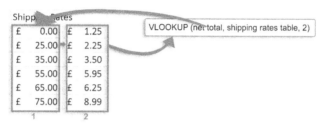

To insert a VLOOKUP, click on the cell you want the calculation to appear in (D12), then go to your formulas ribbon and click 'insert function'.

From the dialog box that appears, select VLOOKUP.

*If the function isn't in the list, type VLOOKUP into the search field and click 'go'.*

Click OK when you're done.

# Chapter 5: Formulas & Functions

In the 'function arguments' dialog box, click in the first argument box, 'lookup value'. This is the value we want to look up in the shipping rates table. In this case the net total is in cell D11, so click D11 to add the cell to the 'lookup value' field.

Next click in the 'table array' field. In this field, we want to specify the table of values we are looking up. In this case the table array is the shipping rates table (highlighted in red, above). So click on F15 and drag your mouse over to G20, to select the table.

Now click in the 'col index num' field. This is the column in the table that contains the values we want to return.

So for example, looking at the shipping rates table, if the net total is under 25, we return 1.25.

If the net total is between 25 and 34, we return 2.25 and so on.

The net total range is column 1 and the shipping rates are column 2. We want to return the shipping rates, so type 2 in the 'col index num' field.

Click OK.

Try adjusting the item prices or number of items and see what happens to the shipping rate.

# Types of Data

There are several different types of data you will come across while using Excel. These data can be numeric such as whole numbers called integers (eg 10), numbers with decimal points (eg 29.93), currencies (eg £4.67 or $43.76), as well as date and time, text and so on.

Going back to our scoring spreadsheet, we need another column for the average scores.

Insert a new column and type the heading 'Average' as shown below.

| | D2 | ▾ | ⋮ | ✕ ✓ $f_x$ | =E2/D2 |

| | A | B 22-Apr | C 29-Apr | D Played | E Total | F Average |
|---|---|---|---|---|---|---|
| 1 | | | | | | |
| 2 | Barbara | 21 | 19 | 2 | 40 | =E2/D2 |
| 3 | Ann | 10 | 21 | 2 | 31 | |
| 4 | Flo | 7 | 7 | 2 | 14 | |
| 5 | Rose | 9 | 12 | 2 | 21 | |
| 6 | Emily | | 0 | 1 | 0 | |
| 7 | Josie | 21 | 21 | 2 | 42 | |
| 8 | Lin | | | 0 | 0 | |
| 9 | Joan | 19 | | 1 | 19 | |
| 10 | Eva | 21 | 14 | 2 | 35 | |

We are going to work out the average scores over the number of games the players have played. In the Cell F2 enter the formula

```
Average = Total Score / Total number of Games Played
```

The total score is in E2 and the total number of games played is in D2.

So we enter into F2:

```
= E2 / D2
```

Use the forward slash for divide:   **/**

Replicate the formula down the column as we did previously in the exercise.

Now the number format isn't as accurate as we want it. We need to tell Excel that the data in this column is a number, accurate to two decimal places.

Highlight the cells you want to apply the number format to, as shown below.

| | A | 22-Apr | 29-Apr | Played | Total | Average |
|---|---|---|---|---|---|---|
| 2 | Barbara | 21 | 19 | 2 | 40 | 20 |
| 3 | Ann | 10 | 21 | 2 | 31 | 15.5 |
| 4 | Flo | 7 | 7 | 2 | 14 | 7 |
| 5 | Rose | 9 | 12 | 2 | 21 | 10.5 |
| 6 | Emily | | 0 | 1 | 0 | 0 |
| 7 | Josie | 21 | 21 | 2 | 42 | 21 |
| 8 | Lin | | | 0 | 0 | 0 |
| 9 | Joan | 19 | | 1 | 19 | 19 |
| 10 | Eva | 21 | 14 | 2 | 35 | 17.5 |

On the home ribbon go up to number format (it will currently say 'general' in box). Click the little arrow next to it.

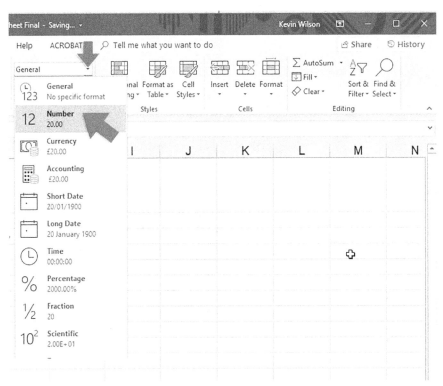

From the drop down menu click number. This will format all the selected cells as a number with 2 decimal places.

It would be the same for recording the fees paid by the players. Insert another column and call it 'fee'. Say the fees are 4.50. When we enter 4.5 into the cell, Excel thinks it's just a number, so we need to tell Excel that it is currency.

Select all the data in the fee column. You don't need to include the heading row.

| | B 22-Apr | C 29-Apr | D Played | E Total | F Average | G Fee |
|---|---|---|---|---|---|---|
| 2 | 21 | 19 | 2 | 40 | 20.00 | 4.5 |
| 3 | 10 | 21 | 2 | 31 | 15.50 | 4.5 |
| 4 | 7 | 7 | 2 | 14 | 7.00 | 4.5 |
| 5 | 9 | 12 | 2 | 21 | 10.50 | 4.5 |
| 6 | | 0 | 1 | 0 | 0.00 | 4.5 |
| 7 | 21 | 21 | 2 | 42 | 21.00 | 4.5 |
| 8 | | | 0 | 0 | 0.00 | 4.5 |
| 9 | 19 | | 1 | 19 | 19.00 | 4.5 |
| 10 | 21 | 14 | 2 | 35 | 17.50 | 4.5 |

On the home ribbon go up to number format (it will currently say 'general' in box). Click the little arrow next to it.

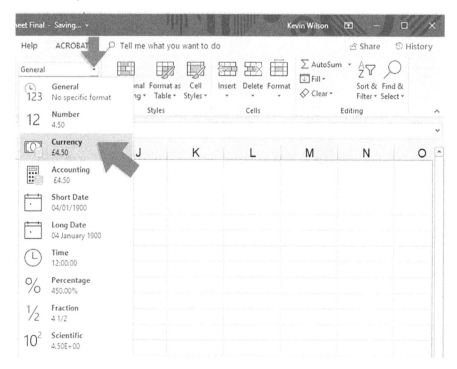

From the drop down menu click currency. This will format all the numbers as a currency.

# Cell Referencing

In Excel, there are two types of cell referencing to think about when copying formulas to other parts of your spreadsheet. Do you want the formula to reference the same cells regardless of where you paste it? Or do you want the cells referenced in the copied formula, to change relative to their new position? You might use absolute cell referencing when referencing a look up table of values, and relative referencing when you want to total up a column or row.

## Relative

Relative cell referencing means that as a formula or function is copied and pasted somewhere else in your spreadsheet, the cell references in the formula or function change to reflect the function's new location.

## Absolute

Absolute cell referencing means that as a formula or function is copied and pasted somewhere else in your spreadsheet, the cell references in the formula or function do not change, they stay fixed on a specific cell.

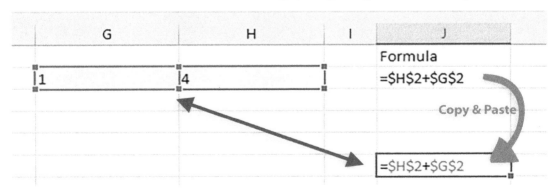

You indicate an absolute cell reference using a dollar sign ($).

Where you put the dollar sign will indicate which row or column is to remain absolute - meaning it doesn't change when you copy the formula.

| | |
|---|---|
| $A$1 | Column & Row do not change when formula is copied to another cell |
| A$1 | Row does not change, but column will change when formula is copied |
| $A1 | Column does not change, but row will change when formula is copied |

All you need to remember is to put the dollar sign before the row or column reference you want to remain the same regardless of where you copy and paste the formula.

# Adding Charts

In this section, we'll take a look at creating charts from our data.

Before we begin, throughout this section, we will be using the resource files.

You can download these files from

www.elluminetpress.com/ms-excel

Go down to the files section and click the icons to download the documents to the documents folder on your PC.

# Types of Chart

There are many different types of charts to choose from, here are a few examples of some common ones.

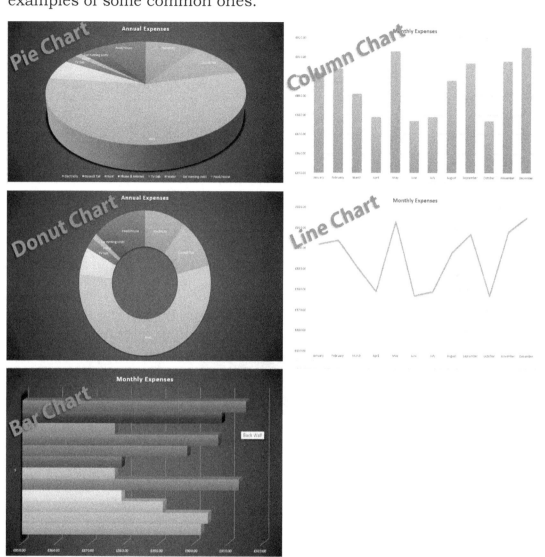

Column and bar charts compare values with each other, line charts show trends over time, donut and pie charts represent proportions of a whole or a percentage.

You will need to use the correct chart for the data you want to represent.

The easiest way to add a chart is to select from your spreadsheet, a column you want for the X-Axis and a column you want for the Y-Axis.

I am going to make a chart on the total scores.

# Creating a Chart

First select all the names in the first column. This will be the X-Axis on the chart.

| | A | B | C | D | E | F | G |
|---|---|---|---|---|---|---|---|
| 1 | | 22-Apr | 29-Apr | Played | Total | Average | Fee |
| 2 | Barbara | 21 | 19 | 2 | 40 | 20.00 | £9.00 |
| 3 | Ann | 10 | 21 | 2 | 31 | 15.50 | £9.00 |
| 4 | Flo | 7 | 7 | 2 | 14 | 7.00 | £9.00 |
| 5 | Rose | 9 | 12 | 2 | 21 | 10.50 | £9.00 |
| 6 | Emily | | 0 | 1 | 0 | 0.00 | £9.00 |
| 7 | Josie | 21 | 21 | 2 | 42 | 21.00 | £9.00 |
| 8 | Lin | | | 0 | 0 | #DIV/0! | £9.00 |
| 9 | Joan | 19 | | 1 | 19 | 19.00 | £9.00 |
| 10 | Eva | 21 | 14 | 2 | 35 | 17.50 | £9.00 |
| 11 | | | | | | | |

Now hold down the control key (ctrl) on your keyboard. This allows you to multi-select.

While holding down control, select the data in the total column with your mouse.

This will be the Y-Axis on the chart. Note the data in the names column is still highlighted.

| E1 | | | | $f_x$ | Total | | |
|---|---|---|---|---|---|---|---|
| | A | B | C | D | E | F | G |
| 1 | | 22-Apr | 29-Apr | Played | Total | Average | Fee |
| 2 | Barbara | 21 | 19 | 2 | 40 | 20.00 | £9.00 |
| 3 | Ann | 10 | 21 | 2 | 31 | 15.50 | £9.00 |
| 4 | Flo | 7 | 7 | 2 | 14 | 7.00 | £9.00 |
| 5 | Rose | 9 | 12 | 2 | 21 | 10.50 | £9.00 |
| 6 | Emily | | 0 | 1 | 0 | 0.00 | £9.00 |
| 7 | Josie | 21 | 21 | 2 | 42 | 21.00 | £9.00 |
| 8 | Lin | | | 0 | 0 | #DIV/0! | £9.00 |
| 9 | Joan | 19 | | 1 | 19 | 19.00 | £9.00 |
| 10 | Eva | 21 | 14 | 2 | 35 | 17.50 | £9.00 |

Release the control key and go to the insert ribbon.

In the centre of the ribbon, you will find some different types of charts – line charts, column charts, pie charts.

I am going for a nice 3D column chart. Click the 3D column chart shown below to select it.

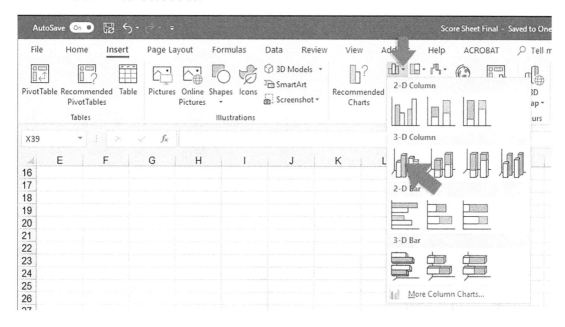

Excel will paste your chart into your spreadsheet.

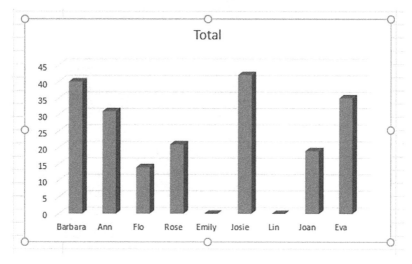

## Chapter 6: Adding Charts

You are automatically taken to the design ribbon where you can select a style to auto-format the chart for you.

Select a style from the options that looks good. To see more styles, click the small arrow to the bottom right of the chart styles box.

I'm going for a nice shaded effect that matches the shading on my table.

# Formatting Charts

You can format and customise the individual chart elements, such as the axis, axis titles, chart title, data labels, gridlines and the legend.

## Chart Titles

Excel will automatically give your chart a title, but more often than not, the title isn't very explanatory.

Click on the automatically generated title on your chart, delete the text then type in your own title, 'Final Scores'.

## Chart Elements

Charts are made up of elements. These could be axes, titles, gridlines, data and so on. To edit the chart elements, click on your chart to select it.

You'll see three icons appear down the right hand edge of the chart. Click on the top one to reveal the slide out menu. From here, you can add axis titles, chart titles, labels, gridlines and a legend, by clicking the tick boxes next to the elements in the list.

# Axis Titles

On some charts, Excel might not have added any axis titles. If this is the case, click your chart then click the chart elements icon, circled below.

In the slide out menu, click the small right arrow next to 'axis titles'. From the slide out, click both 'primary horizontal' and 'primary vertical', for both X and Y axis on your chart.

To change the text in the axis titles, click on the title, delete the text and type in your titles. In this example, the horizontal axis is 'player name' and the vertical axis is 'final score'.

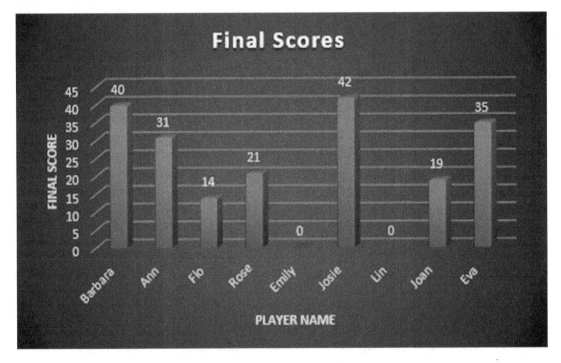

# Customising Charts

There are shortcuts to changing elements of your chart, but to give you the most control over the changes, we'll do it this way.

Right click on a blank space on your chart and from the popup menu, click 'format chart area'.

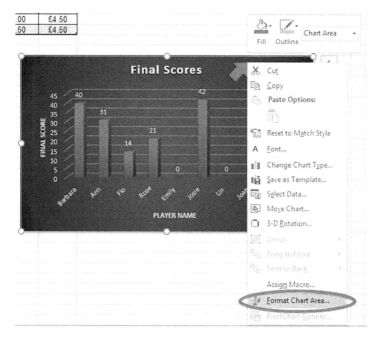

In the side panel that appears, you have a number of options.

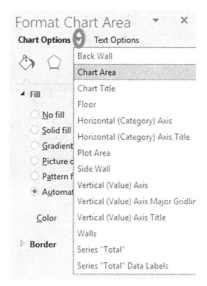

Click the small down arrow next to 'chart options' to open the drop down menu.

## Chapter 6: Adding Charts

Here you can select the element of the chart you want to customise (chart colour, labels, and so on).

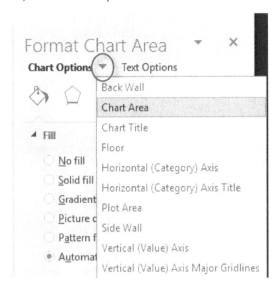

Each option on the menu will change a specific part of your chart. In the illustration below, you can see each part of the chart corresponds to an option on the menu.

Chart title, horizontal axis, vertical axis, and so on. If you want to change the chart area colour, select 'chart area', if you want to change the axis titles, select axis title from the menu, and so on.

# Change Background to Solid Colour

To change the background colour, right click on a blank space on your chart and from the popup menu, click 'format chart area'.

In this example, we want to change the background colour. The background is called the 'chart area', so make sure 'chart area' is selected.

To change to a solid colour, expand the fill section by clicking on the small down arrow next to fill. Click 'solid fill', then click the down arrow next to the paint pot, and select a colour.

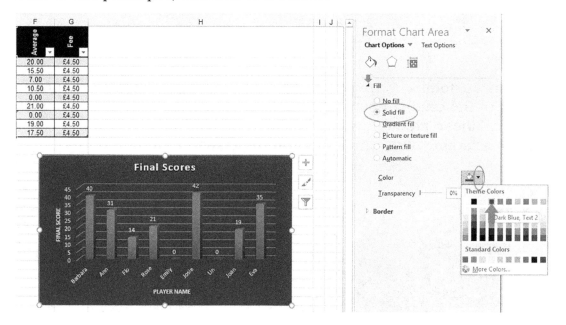

# Change Background to Gradient Colour

You can also apply a gradient colour, meaning one colour blends into another over the surface of your chart.

To do this, right click on your chart, click 'format chart'. From the chart options make sure 'chart area' is selected as in the previous section, except from the fill options, click 'gradient fill'.

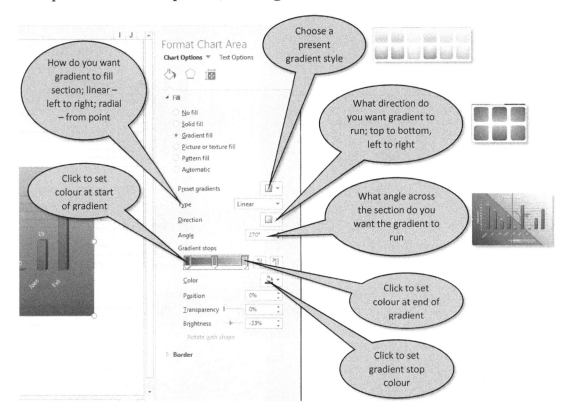

You can customise your gradient. Take a closer look at the bottom section of the gradient settings. You can choose from several gradient presets. Linear gradients run left to right or top to bottom. Radial gradients radiate out from a point on the chart.

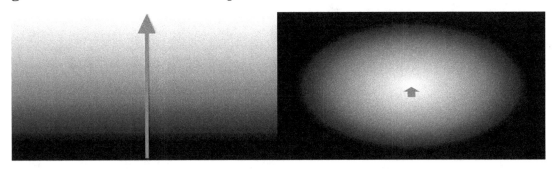

You can select the type of gradient from the 'type' drop down field.

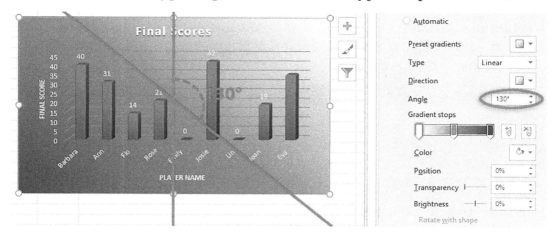

You can also set the angle at which the gradient runs. This only applies to linear gradients and sets the angle at which the colour begins to change. As you can see in the example above, the angle is set to 130° which means 130° from the vertical axis shown in red.

Each stop on the gradient bar represents a colour. You can change these colours by clicking on the stop, then selecting the paint pot. From the popup dialog box, click a colour.

For each of the stops, you can change the position of the gradient (where the colour blends), as well as the brightness and transparency of the colour gradient.

# Change Chart Type

To change your chart type, eg from a column chart to a bar chart, click on your chart and select the design ribbon. From the design ribbon, click 'change chart type'.

From the popup dialog box, look down the left hand side for the types of chart you want (pie, bar, line, etc), and select one.

From the right hand pane, select the style of chart you want.

For this example, I am going to choose a nice colourful bar chart.

# Move and Resize Charts

To resize, click on a blank section of your chart. You'll notice some small white dots appear around the chart. These are called resize handles. Drag the resize handles across your page to the size you want the chart.

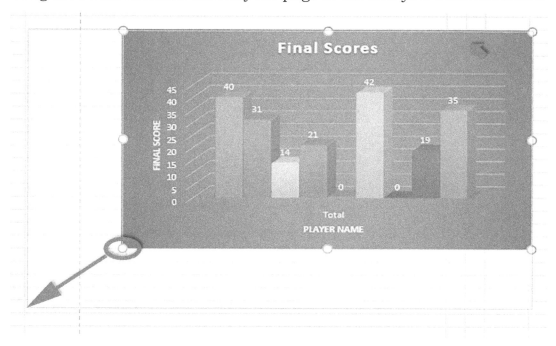

To move your chart into position, click in a blank section of your chart, then drag it with your mouse into a new position.

# Data Analysis

In this section, we'll take a look analysing our data with goal seek, scenario manager, slicers, and pivot tables.

Before we begin, throughout this section, we will be using the resource files.

You can download these files from

www.elluminetpress.com/ms-excel

Go down to the files section and click the icons to download the documents to the documents folder on your PC.

# Goal Seek

Goal seek allows you start with the desired result, the goal in other words, and calculates the value required to give you that result.

For this example, use the **goal seek** worksheet in the **Data Analysis Starter.xlsx** workbook.

Say we want to take out a loan of £10,000. This particular bank has an interest rate of 3.3%. We're paying the loan off over 60 months with a payment of £181.02. We can afford to pay off £200 per month. We can use goal seek to find out how many months we'll be paying the loan off.

First click the monthly payment (cell C4), because this is what we want to change. From the data ribbon, click 'what-if analysis'. From the drop down menu, click 'goal seek'.

On the dialog box that appears, click in 'to value' and enter 200. This is our target amount or goal.

Now we want to achieve this goal by changing the payback duration, so click in 'by changing cell' on the dialog box, then click the cell with the number of months (C4 in this case).

Click OK. We have an answer... It would take 54 months at £200 a month.

| | A | B | C | D | E |
|---|---|---|---|---|---|
| 1 | Loan Amount | £ 10,000.00 | £10,000.00 | | |
| 2 | Interest Rate | 3.3% | 3.3% | | |
| 3 | | | | | |
| 4 | Payback Duration (months) | 60 | 54 | | |
| 5 | Monthly Payments | £181.02 | £200.00 | | |
| 6 | | | | | |
| 7 | Total amount payable | £ 10,861.39 | £10,772.61 | | |

Goal Seek Status

Goal Seeking with Cell C5 found a solution.

Target value: 200
Current value: £200.00

# Data Analysis with Scenario Manager

When creating spreadsheets, you will probably want to explore "what-if" scenarios and see how different values effect results. Say we were running a small bookstore. We bought in some books and we want to see what our sales revenue and profit will be for different prices to help us price our books.

For this example, use the **scenario manager** worksheet in the **Data Analysis Starter.xlsx** workbook.

## Creating Scenarios

To add a scenario, go to your data ribbon and click 'what-if analysis'. From the drop down menu, select 'scenario manager'.

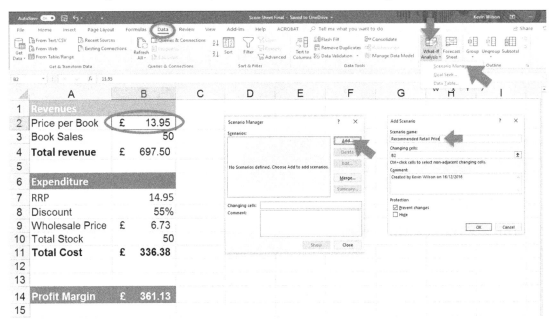

From the dialog box that appears, click add. Then from the 'add scenario' dialog box, type in a meaningful name in the field 'scenario name'.

Click in the 'changing cells' field underneath, then click the cell or cells you want to change. In this case we want to change the price per book in cell B2. So click B2.

Click OK.

Repeat the process and create scenarios for 'Sale Price' at £10.95, and 'Give Away' price at £8.99

Now in the scenario manager dialog box, you'll have three scenarios you can click on, and instantly see the results.

Click on one of the scenarios then click show.

| Recommended Retail Price | | |
| --- | --- | --- |
| **Revenues** | | |
| Price per Book | £ | 14.95 |
| Book Sales | | 50 |
| **Total revenue** | £ | 747.50 |
| | | |
| **Expenditure** | | |
| RRP | | 14.95 |
| Discount | | 55% |
| Wholesale Price | £ | 6.73 |
| Total Stock | | 50 |
| **Total Cost** | £ | 336.38 |
| | | |
| **Profit Margin** | £ | 411.13 |

| Sale Price | | |
| --- | --- | --- |
| **Revenues** | | |
| Price per Book | £ | 10.95 |
| Book Sales | | 50 |
| **Total revenue** | £ | 547.50 |
| | | |
| **Expenditure** | | |
| RRP | | 14.95 |
| Discount | | 55% |
| Wholesale Price | £ | 6.73 |
| Total Stock | | 50 |
| **Total Cost** | £ | 336.38 |
| | | |
| **Profit Margin** | £ | 211.13 |

| Give Away Price | | |
| --- | --- | --- |
| **Revenues** | | |
| Price per Book | £ | 8.99 |
| Book Sales | | 50 |
| **Total revenue** | £ | 449.50 |
| | | |
| **Expenditure** | | |
| RRP | | 14.95 |
| Discount | | 55% |
| Wholesale Price | £ | 6.73 |
| Total Stock | | 50 |
| **Total Cost** | £ | 336.38 |
| | | |
| **Profit Margin** | £ | 113.13 |

If you need to edit any of the scenarios, just click on the name in the scenario list and click edit. You'll be able to go through the add scenario process again and amend the values.

# Summary Reports

You can also generate quick reports of your scenarios. To do this, go to your scenario manager.

Data Ribbon -> What-If Analysis -> Scenario Manager

From the scenario manager dialog box, click 'summary'.

On the scenario summary dialog box, click 'scenario summary', to produce a report.

For the 'result cells', this is the cell or cells we're looking at when we're changing the values in the scenarios.

We want to show how changing the price per book affects profit margin. So here, select B14 because this is where the value for profit margin is.

If we wanted to show how changing the price per book affects total revenue, we'd select the total revenue value in B4.

Click OK.

Here you can see Excel has created a new worksheet with our report on.

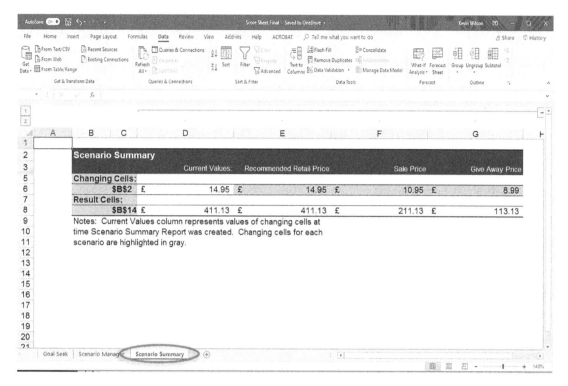

If you look at the report, some labels aren't really that clear, 'changing cells' or 'result cells' don't really tell us much. Good practice is to change these to more meaningful names.

To do this, just delete the text in the cells you want to rename then type in your own, as shown below.

| Scenario Summary | | Current Values: | Recommended Retail Price | | Sale Price | | Give Away Price |
|---|---|---|---|---|---|---|---|
| Scenarios | £ | 14.95 | £ | 14.95 | £ | 10.95 | £ 8.99 |
| Profit Margins | £ | 411.13 | £ | 411.13 | £ | 211.13 | £ 113.13 |

Notes: Current Values column represents values of changing cells at time Scenario Summary Report was created. Changing cells for each scenario are highlighted in gray.

This now makes a bit more sense.

# Creating Pivot Tables

A pivot table is a data summarisation tool and can automatically sort, count, total or average the data stored in one table or worksheet and display the results in a new table or worksheet. Reports can then be produced to present the data.

With a pivot table you can quickly pivot data, meaning you reorganise or summarise the data. Pivoting data can help you answer different scenarios, for example, best selling products, sales channels and so on.

For this example, use the **pivot table data** worksheet in the **Data Analysis Starter.xlsx** workbook.

First click in any cell in the data table. This is to indicate to Excel what table of data it should use to create the pivot table.

From the insert ribbon, click 'pivot table'. Make sure Excel has selected the correct range in the 'select a table or range' field. Excel will indicate the selection with a dashed line around the data.

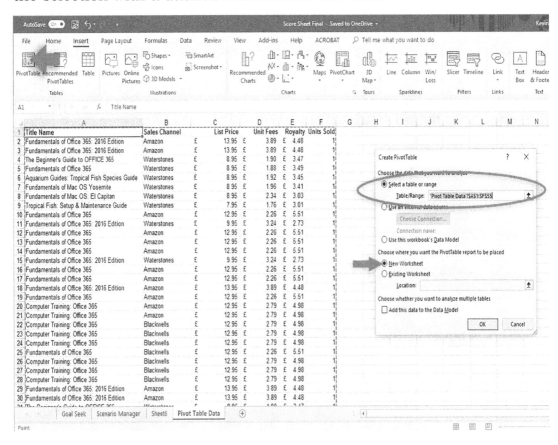

Next, in the dialog box, select 'new worksheet'. Click OK.

You'll see your 'PivotTable Fields' sidebar open on the right hand side.

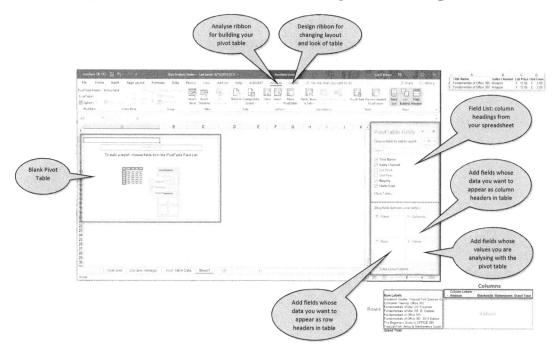

From here we can start building pivot tables. You can add and remove fields. You can drag the fields over to the rows box or the columns box, on the bottom half of the 'PivotTable Fields' sidebar, depending on how you want to analyse your data. Any field you drag to the rows box will appear down the left hand side of the table and anything you drag to the columns box will appear as columns across the top of your table. This makes up the row and column headers of the pivot table.

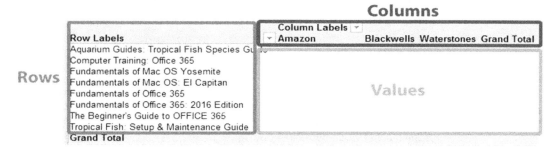

The values box, is the data you want to analyse against the rows and column headers. So, in the example above, our rows are the book titles and the columns are the sales channels.

In the values section, we could add the 'royalty' field to see how much income is generated for each title in each sales channel. Or we could add 'units sold' to the values section to see how many books have sold in each sales channel.

So lets build a pivot table. In this example, we want to find the total income per sales channel.

First add the rows. This will be title name. Either click and drag 'title name' to the 'rows' box, or click the tick next to 'title name'

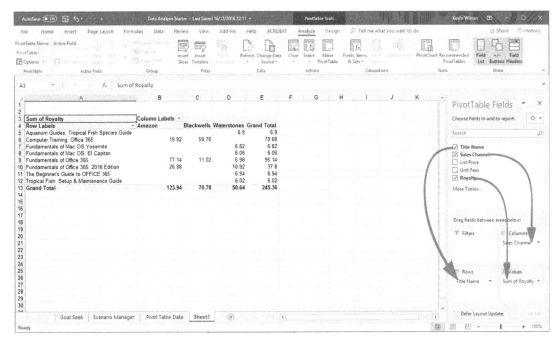

Next we need to add some values. We want the income, in this case income is labelled 'royalty'. So click the tick box next to the 'royalty' field. You can also drag the 'royalty' field over to the 'values' box.

Now we should have a list of books and their total royalties. This is the total income for all sales channels.

| Row Labels | Sum of Royalty |
|---|---|
| Aquarium Guides: Tropical Fish Species Guide | 6.9 |
| Computer Training: Office 365 | 79.68 |
| Fundamentals of Mac OS Yosemite | 6.82 |
| Fundamentals of Mac OS: El Capitan | 6.06 |
| Fundamentals of Office 365 | 95.14 |
| Fundamentals of Office 365: 2016 Edition | 37.8 |
| The Beginner's Guide to OFFICE 365 | 6.94 |
| Tropical Fish: Setup & Maintenance Guide | 6.02 |
| Grand Total | 245.36 |

The next step is to add the sales channels. We want the royalties to be split into columns, one for each sales channel.

So to do this, click and drag the 'sales channel' field over to the 'columns' box.

Now we can see the royalties for each sales channel - Amazon, Blackwells and Waterstones, as well as grand totals. In this case Amazon generated the highest revenue (£123.94).

| Sum of Royalty | Column Labels ▾ | | | |
| --- | --- | --- | --- | --- |
| Row Labels ▾ | Amazon | Blackwells | Waterstones | Grand Total |
| Aquarium Guides: Tropical Fish Species Guide | | | 6.9 | 6.9 |
| Computer Training: Office 365 | 19.92 | 59.76 | | 79.68 |
| Fundamentals of Mac OS Yosemite | | | 6.82 | 6.82 |
| Fundamentals of Mac OS: El Capitan | | | 6.06 | 6.06 |
| Fundamentals of Office 365 | 77.14 | 11.02 | 6.98 | 95.14 |
| Fundamentals of Office 365: 2016 Edition | 26.88 | | 10.92 | 37.8 |
| The Beginner's Guide to OFFICE 365 | | | 6.94 | 6.94 |
| Tropical Fish: Setup & Maintenance Guide | | | 6.02 | 6.02 |
| Grand Total | 123.94 | 70.78 | 50.64 | 245.36 |

How about the number of books sold? We can answer this question by adding the 'units sold' field.

This might be a bit confusing to read. To make the data analysis easier, Excel has a feature called slicers.

# Using Slicers

A slicer is essentially a filter, and allows you to filter the data in the pivot table to make things easier to analyse.

In the above example, we can see both units sold and the royalties for each sales channel, all on one table. To make things easier to analyse, we can add a slicer for sales channels that will enable us to select a sales channel, and display a pivot table for only that channel.

This helps break your data down into more concise parts.

To insert a slicer, click any cell in your pivot table, go to the analyse ribbon and click 'insert slicer'.

From the 'insert slicers' panel that opens up, click the field you want to organise the data by. In this example we are organising the data by sales channel, so click 'sales channel'.

You'll see a slicer pop up with three sales channels, Amazon, Blackwells and Waterstones.

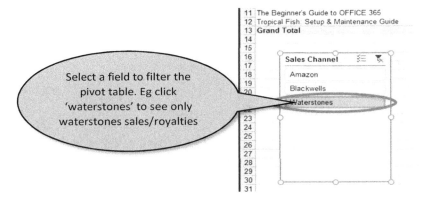

You can select multiple selections in the slicer by holding down the control key while you click.

Now, you'll see your slicer appear on your worksheet.

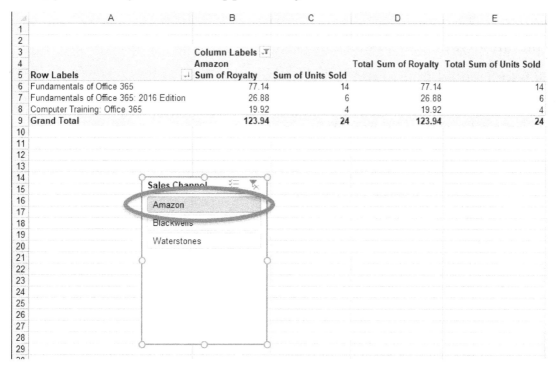

If you select 'amazon' you'll see all sales, etc from the amazon channel. Similarly if you select 'blackwells' or 'waterstones' you'll see sales from those channels.

If you select all of the channels - remember hold down the control key on your keyboard to select multiple options - you'll see sales from all channels.

# Sorting Pivot Table Data

You can also sort data in these tables in the same way you'd sort any column in your spreadsheet.

Say we wanted to find the best selling book?

I can adjust my pivot table to show total books sold (just need 'title name' and 'units sold' fields).

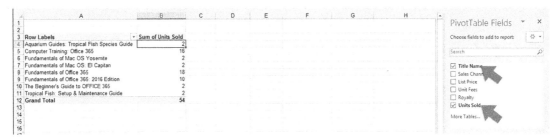

Now click in the 'sum of units sold' field, in the pivot table.

| Row Labels | Sum of Units Sold |
| --- | --- |
| Aquarium Guides: Tropical Fish Species Guide | 2 |
| Computer Training: Office 365 | |
| Fundamentals of Mac OS Yosemite | |
| Fundamentals of Mac OS: El Capitan | 2 |
| Fundamentals of Office 365 | 18 |
| Fundamentals of Office 365: 2016 Edition | 10 |
| The Beginner's Guide to OFFICE 365 | 2 |
| Tropical Fish: Setup & Maintenance Guide | 2 |
| Grand Total | 54 |

Go to your data ribbon and click the 'descending' sort icon.

We can see the best seller is 'Fundamentals of Office 365'.

| Row Labels | Sum of Units Sold |
| --- | --- |
| Fundamentals of Office 365 | 18 |
| Computer Training: Office 365 | 16 |
| Fundamentals of Office 365: 2016 Edition | 10 |
| Tropical Fish: Setup & Maintenance Guide | 2 |
| The Beginner's Guide to OFFICE 365 | 2 |
| Fundamentals of Mac OS Yosemite | 2 |
| Aquarium Guides: Tropical Fish Species Guide | 2 |
| Fundamentals of Mac OS: El Capitan | 2 |
| Grand Total | 54 |

# Pivot Charts

Pivot charts are pretty much the same thing as regular charts, covered earlier, except they represent data in a pivot table rather than a regular worksheet.

You add your charts in a similar fashion. First click on your pivot table and from the analyse ribbon, click 'pivot chart'.

From the dialog box that appears, select a chart that is most appropriate for the data you are trying to illustrate. You can choose from pie charts, column or bar charts and line charts.

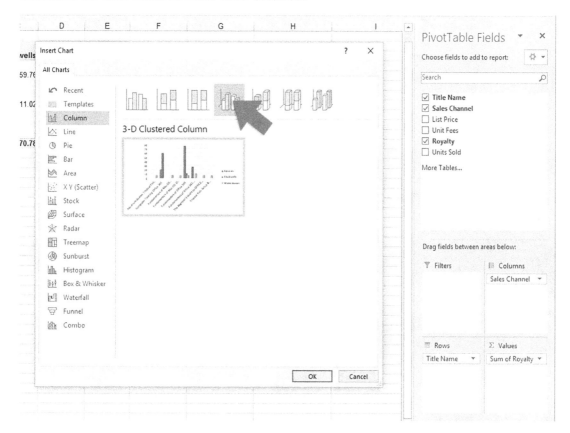

For this example, I'm going to add a nice 3D column chart.

As you can see from the chart, things can be a bit difficult to read on this particular chart. All three sales channels are on the same chart.

It would be nice if we can view them separately. Excel allows you to use slicers, which is essentially a filter.

In this example I am going to filter the chart by sales channel. So from the analyse ribbon, click 'insert slicer'. From the dialog box that appears, select sales channel and click OK.

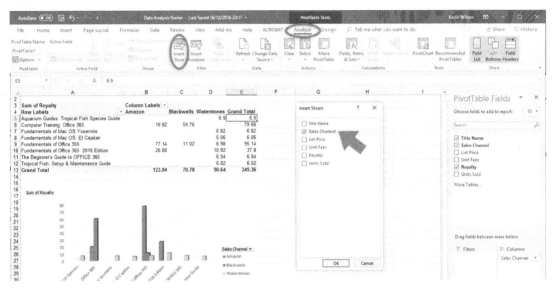

In the popup box that appears, I can select each of my sales channels in turn and take a closer look at the sales data.

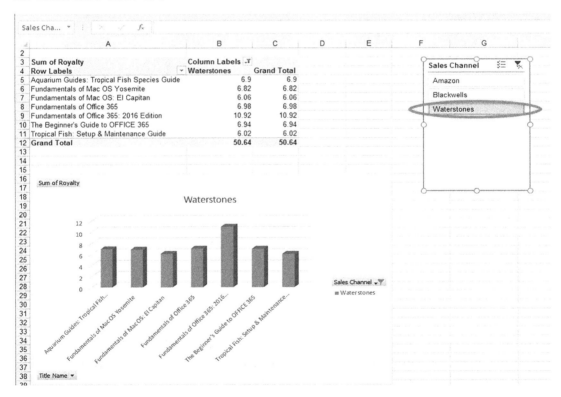

Try experimenting with adding different fields to different boxes on the 'PivotTable Fields' sidebar and see how it affects the pivot table.

You might have something like this...

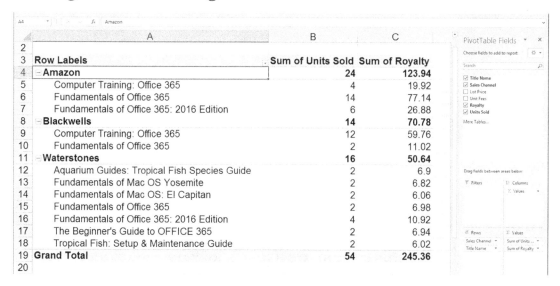

Notice where the fields are on the bottom half of the 'PivotTable Fields' sidebar in relation to the pivot chart.

Give it a try.

# Data Validation

In this section, we'll take a look data validation rules to make sure users enter valid data into the spreadsheet.

Before we begin, throughout this section, we will be using the resource files.

You can download these files from

`www.elluminetpress.com/ms-excel`

Go down to the files section and click the icons to download the documents to the documents folder on your PC.

# Validation Rules

In Excel, you can set a variety of rules to cells to help users enter the correct data.

Lets take a look at an example in the **Data Validation Demo.xlsx** workbook.

## By Data Type

Whole numbers are called integers in Excel and do not have any decimal places. In the example, we can add a validation check to the 'number of items' column. It's safe to assume that these will only be whole numbers, don't think anyone will try order half an LED torch light.

Select the cells to apply the validation check to. Go to your data ribbon and click 'data validation'

From the dialog box, click the drop down box under 'allow' and select 'whole number', because we only want to allow whole numbers in these cells.

You can also set a criteria for the whole numbers. For example, we could set a range 1 - 500. We could argue that you can't order 0 items on the order form and set a maximum limit of only shipping 500 at a time. So in the data field, select 'between'. Set the minimum value to 1 and the max value to 500.

If there was no maximum limit to the number of items ordered. Instead of selecting 'between' in the data field, you could select 'greater than or equal to' and set the minimum value to 1.

# Text Length

You can enforce a specific length of text or numbers with data validation. In our example, we have a field called SKU, this is a unique product code each product in our catalogue has to identify it. In this case, each SKU is exactly 5 digits long and can't be more than 5 or less than 5 digits.

Select the cells you want to apply the validation to, in this example, it's the SKU column.

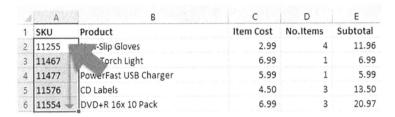

Go to your data ribbon and select 'data validation'.

From the dialog box, in the 'allow' field, select 'text length'.

In the 'data' field, select 'equal to', because we want the text length equal to a certain length.

In the 'length' field, select 5. We want the length of the entries to be equal to 5 characters long.

Now when you try type in a number that has more or less than 5 characters, you will get an error message.

# Displaying Messages

You can display messages to your users if they input invalid data and messages explaining what data is required.

If we take a look at an example in the **Data Validation Demo.xlsx** workbook

## Input Message

Input messages appear, telling the user what data is expected, when the cell is selected.

Going back to our example, remember we added a validation check to the 'number of items' column to accept whole numbers between 1 and 500. We can add an input message to explain this to the user.

To do this, select the cells in the 'number of items' column.

From the data ribbon click 'data validation'.

From the dialog box go to the 'input message' tab.

Check the check box next to 'Show input message when cell is selected', so the message appears when the user clicks on one of the cells.

## Chapter 8: Data Validation

In the title field enter a title. This could be the name of the column.

In the 'input message' field, enter the message. This is a brief description of the field and the data that is required from the user.

Click OK when you're done.

When the user clicks on a cell, they'll see the message pop up.

| SKU | Product | Item Cost | No.Items | Subtotal |
|-----|---------|-----------|----------|----------|
| 11255 | Non-Slip Gloves | 2.99 | 4 | 11.96 |
| 11467 | LED Torch Light | 6.99 | | |
| 11477 | PowerFast USB Charger | 5.99 | | |
| 11576 | CD Labels | 4.50 | | |
| 11554 | DVD+R 16x 10 Pack | 6.99 | | |
| | | | | |
| | | | Net Total | 59.41 |
| | | | Shipping Method | Standard |
| | | | Shipping Cost | 2.99 |
| | | | Total | 62.40 |

No. Items
Enter the number of items customer has ordered of this item. Entered values must be between 1 and 500.

# Error Messages

If the user enters invalid data, you can alert then using an error message.

If we take a look at an example in the **Data Validation Demo.xlsx** workbook

To do this, select the cells in the 'number of items' column.

From the data ribbon click 'data validation'.

From the dialog box that appears click the 'error alert' tab.

Click the check box next to 'Show error alert after invalid data is entered', so the message appears when the user clicks on one of the cells.

In the title field enter a title. This could be the name of the column.

In the 'error message' field, enter the message. This is the message you want to display to the user, type a reminder in here as to what data is expected for that cell.

In the style field. Select the type of error message you want to show. An error, warning or an info box. You have Stop, Warning and Info as shown below.

Click OK when you're done. If the user enters invalid data, they'll see the dialog box pop up.

# Create a Drop Down List

Drop down lists allow the user to select pre-set options allocated to a particular cell, instead of having to type the data in.

If we take a look at an example in the **Data Validation Demo.xlsx** workbook

To create a drop down list, select the cell you want the drop down list to appear in.

From the Data tab, click the Data Validation.

From the dialog box that appears, in the allow field, click in the drop down, and from the options select 'list'.

Click in the 'source' field that appears, and select the range of values that you want the user to be able to choose from, in the drop down box we're creating. Click OK when you're done

You'll notice a little down arrow appear next to the cell we selected. Click the arrow to select the desired option and see what happens.

# Locking Cells

When your users are using your spreadsheet, they may accidentally wipe out formulas and cells you don't really want them to change.

Excel allows you to lock cells and cell ranges so your users can't change the contents.

If we take a look at an example in the **Data Validation Demo.xlsx** workbook, it would make the spreadsheet more resilient to errors if we locked all the cells with formulas, shipping data, and totals, so the user can't change them.

If you click on 'protect sheet' in the review ribbon, Excel will by default protect all the cells in your spreadsheet. This isn't quite what we want, so we need to tell Excel which cells the user will be able to change.

To do this, select the cells the user is allowed to enter data. In the example, this would be: SKU, Product, Item Cost, No. Items and the shipping option. So highlight these cells.

Right click on the selection and select 'format cells', then go to the 'protection' tab. Click the check box next to 'locked' to remove it. This will unlock the selected cells.

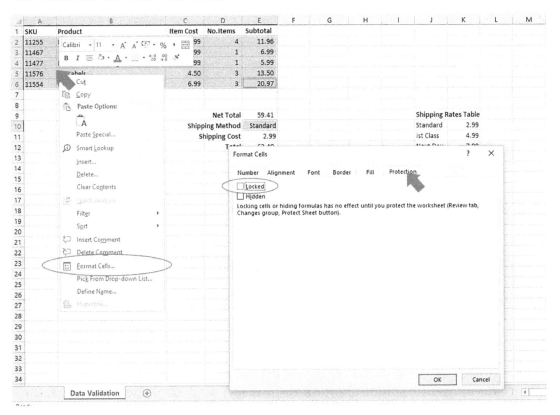

Now go to the review ribbon and select 'protect sheet'.

From the dialog box, you can enter a password to allow users to unlock the sheet temporarily, or leave it blank if not. Below that, you can assign different permissions to the user if you want them to be able to add rows, delete rows or be able to sort. Just click the check boxes next to the options in the list to enable them.

Now, when a user tries to edit a protected cell, they will get an error message.

| B | C | D | E | F | G | H | I | J | K | L |
|---|---|---|---|---|---|---|---|---|---|---|
| Product | Item Cost | No.Items | Subtotal | | | | | | | |
| Non-Slip Gloves | 2.99 | 4 | 11.96 | | | | | | | |
| LED Torch Light | 6.99 | 1 | 6.99 | | | | | | | |
| PowerFast USB Charger | 5.99 | 1 | 5.99 | | | | | | | |
| CD Labels | 4.50 | 3 | 13.50 | | | | | | | |
| DVD+R 16x 10 Pack | 6.99 | 3 | 20.97 | | | | | | | |

Microsoft Excel   ✕

⚠ The cell or chart you're trying to change is on a protected sheet. To make a change, unprotect the sheet. You might be requested to enter a password.

OK

# Resources

To help you understand the procedures and concepts explored in this book, we have developed some video resources and app demos for you to use, as you work through the book.

To find the resources, open your web browser and navigate to the following website

`www.elluminetpress.com/ms-excel`

At the beginning of each chapter, you'll find a website that contains the resources for that chapter.

# File Resources

To save the files into your OneDrive documents folder, right click on the icons above and select 'save target as' (or 'save link as', on some browsers). In the dialog box that appears, select 'OneDrive', click the 'Documents' folder, then click 'save'.

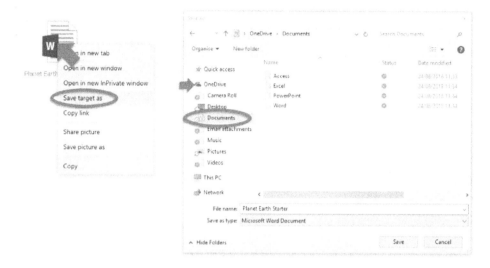

The sample images are stored in a compressed zip file. To download the zip file, right click on the zip icon on the page above, 'Sample Images. zip. Select 'save target as' (or 'save link as', on some browsers) and save it into 'pictures' on your OneDrive folder.

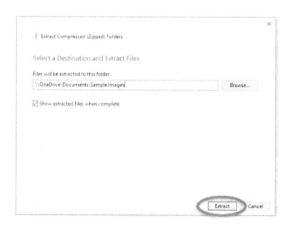

Once you have downloaded the zip file, go to your 'pictures' folder in your OneDrive, right click on the zip file, and select 'extract all' from the menu. From the dialog box that appears click 'extract'. This will create a new folder in your pictures called 'sample images'. You'll find the images used in the examples in the books.

# Video Resources

The video resources are grouped into sections for each chapter in the book. Click the thumbnail link to open the section.

Getting Started

Building Documents

Managing Documents

Images, Tables & Charts

Document Templates

When you open the link to the video resources, you'll see a thumbnail list at the bottom.

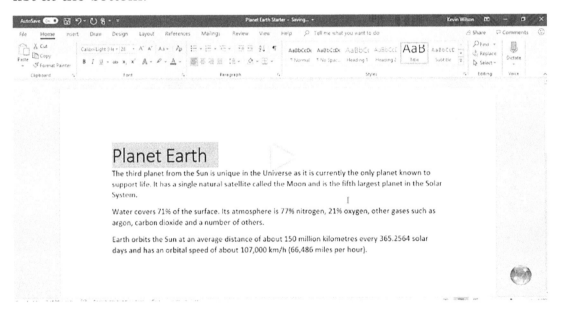

Click on the thumbnail for the particular video you want to watch. Most videos are between 30 and 60 seconds outlining the procedure, others are a bit longer.

Share video on social media

Run video in full screen mode

Previous video, pause, next video

Video progress bar. Use to skip to different points in video

Set video playback speed

When the video is playing, hover your mouse over the video and you'll see some controls...

# Index

# Index

005.54 WILS
Wilson, Kevin,
Using Excel 2019 :

MAY 1 1 2021

9 781913 151034